THE POWER OF
Quick and Frequent
Practice

Joyful Small Moves with Big Impacts on Elementary Literacy

TAMMY MULLIGAN

Routledge
Taylor & Francis Group

NEW YORK AND LONDON

A Stenhouse Book

Designed cover image: Getty Images

First published 2025
by Routledge
605 Third Avenue, New York, NY 10158

and by Routledge
4 Park Square, Milton Park, Abingdon, Oxon, OX14 4RN

Routledge is an imprint of the Taylor & Francis Group, an informa business

© 2025 Tammy Mulligan

ISBN: 9781032820996 (pbk)
ISBN: 9781003502920 (ebk)

DOI: 10.4324/9781003502920

Typeset in Times New Roman
by KnowledgeWorks Global Ltd.

"In *The Power of Quick and Frequent Practice: Joyful Small Moves with Big Impacts on Elementary Literacy*, Tammy takes the essential components of robust reading instruction and breaks them down into student-focused, effective, and manageable systems. From targeted phonics instruction to collaborative comprehension conversations, you'll learn how to use every moment of your teaching day wisely and with purpose. Whether you're new to the profession or a seasoned educator seeking fresh inspiration, you can rely on Tammy's wisdom and practical strategies to elevate your literacy teaching."

—**Maria Walther,** *Literacy Consultant and Co-Author of* A Year for the Books *and* The Literacy Workshop

"Tammy's honest reflections about her teaching journey and her suggestions of 'small moves' within our instruction left me feeling empowered. She reassures readers of the importance of their own data collection and offers valuable suggestions for creating manageable systems that will enable teachers to meet the needs of all students in all areas of instruction."

—**Mandy Robek,** *elementary educator*

"*The Power of Quick and Frequent Practice* by Tammy Mulligan is exactly what teachers need right now. It's the book I wish I had when I was a new classroom teacher, and the book I longed for when I'd been teaching for a while and felt stuck and in need of a fresh perspective. It's the book I will now recommend to other educators who want to build more targeted, responsive practice opportunities into their routines and/or partner with families in more authentic ways, but don't know where to begin, are frustrated by failed attempts, or feel like there isn't time to do this work in an already overcrowded school day. On every page, in such a clear and conversational way, Tammy shares the experiences of her current classroom and invites each reader to take what she offers and make it their own. This book is pure gold and I'm so grateful to Tammy for sharing it with all of us."

—**Gwen Blumberg,** *Literacy Leader*

"Tammy Mulligan is a breath of fresh air when it comes to teaching readers. Tammy has developed structures to help students develop independence and teachers manage meeting the different needs of each child. No matter how long you've been teaching, you'll be glad to use Tammy's ideas in your classroom."

—**Ruth Ayres,** *Director of The Lead Learners (a professional learning community) and Editor in Chief of* Choice Literacy

To the kids at Hanscom School on Hanscom
Air Force Base.

Thank you for letting me learn alongside you and for bringing so
much joy into the classroom. I am so grateful for your perseverance,
enduring spirits, and the community we built together.

contents

acknowledgments

The field of education has been very good to me for the last thirty-four years, and I have stood on the shoulders of countless educators who were so generous to share their classrooms with me and let me learn alongside them as we experimented with teaching practices together.

To Brenda Power—Thank you for always believing that I had something to say, even when I didn't believe in myself. You helped me understand how to bring my voice out on the page and revise my repetitive sentences. You saw how to weave the children's stories throughout this book, and you made the idea feel so doable. I left our writing conference motivated to do more. You gave me one of the dearest gifts I have ever received—the belief that I am a writer.

To Ruth Ayres—Every time you looked at my writing, you found something to admire, whether it was at a writing retreat in person, online, or in Google comments. You saw my writing in its roughest forms, and you helped me to persevere, despite my frequent requests for you to just "take it away and cut it up into articles." Instead, you consolidated the work into one document, created a to-do list, and kept track of my word count—urging me to say more. You encouraged me to seek out a publisher, despite my misgivings. Thank you for giving me your time and your expertise.

To my writing group at Choice Literacy—I can't thank you enough for reading my very early drafts before I even thought they could be a book. Your thoughtfulness helped me see things in my writing that I didn't realize were there.

To Kassia Omohundro Wedekind—Thank you for first reading my manuscript and telling me that it was in "really good shape." Those words made all the future revisions and edits feel doable. Then, you calmly walked me

through each next step, showing me how to get this book over the finish line. The ideas in the book are much clearer thanks to you.

To Sasha Stavsky—I am forever grateful for our collaboration. Our daily talks about kids help me choose teaching points, refine my instruction, and keep perspective about the progress students are making. Everything you touch is infused with joy and laughter, and I am so grateful to spend my days teaching alongside you.

To Andrea Defina—Thank you for being a mentor to me. You helped me reenter the classroom after being away from it for so long. You showed me how to build a community with students and handle all of the unexpected situations that come a teacher's way. I am so grateful for our friendship and our collaboration. I'll never forget our first days together culling our classroom libraries. It was then that you put the books from Responsive Classroom in my hands. You knew just what I needed.

To Kyoko Feeney—I knew I hit the lottery when we were placed in the classroom together. Each week, you bring the Quick and Frequent Individual Plan to life. You gently sit beside young readers and help them practice the necessary skills in quick bursts. Then you watch, listen, notice, and document all that you see. Your insights into how children learn and what they need next are invaluable. I learn so much as I watch the gentle, kind, and clear ways you interact with students.

To Jeanne Goranson—Although we don't get to collaborate as much as I would like any more, I will be forever grateful for the days we worked together in the classroom, talking, thinking, and planning what to do to support each learner. I admire how you help children build stamina and become self-sustaining readers.

To the Lincoln Public Schools, and especially Jessica Rose, Becky McFall, Julie Vincentsen, and Erich Ledebuhr—Thank you for hiring me during the pandemic and making it possible for me to spend my days alongside children. I am forever grateful to you for helping me transition back into the classroom.

To George, my husband and best friend—Thank you for dealing with my intensity for the last thirty-three years. You spend lots of your days listening to my stories from the classroom even though that is probably not your preferred topic of conversation. Thank you for helping me have balance in my life. You are so much fun and each day you give me perspective about what really matters.

To my daughter Abigail—Thank you for always asking about my work and this book, and then for listening. Your constant encouragement to keep going helped me push through. Your caring spirit is in my heart each day.

To my son Connor—Watching you grow has been one of the greatest gifts of my life. I am in awe of your perspectives on life and how they guide you to forge your own path.

To Ranger, Hops, and LuLu—my three dogs. This book would not have happened without you. I needed you there sitting on the couch with me as I wrote. I know my constant fidgeting and getting up for endless cups of tea disturbed your sleep. Thanks for sticking with me.

To Henrietta Yelle—Thank you for being the dearest friend ever and for helping get through those references. You know how much such detailed work terrifies me, and I appreciate you jumping in.

To the Hanscom families—Thank you for sharing your children with me. Each day when the children sing to begin our day, I think how lucky I am to spend my day with your children.

To Melanie Moy and the production team at Stenhouse/Routledge—you for all of your work behind the scenes to take these words in Google Docs and transform them into a beautiful book. I know many careful hours were spent creating, checking, formatting, and editing, and I am forever grateful.

To the teachers who may read this book—When the days get long and the problems mount, please remember that what you do matters. Your work changes lives.

Introduction

It is only a few weeks into the school year, and I am sitting at a grade-level team meeting with the reading team. Our job is to review the literacy screening assessment data results for each classroom. I hold my breath as we move through the spreadsheets for each classroom. The group looks carefully at the data display of the first three classrooms in the grade level. These displays are a scramble of colors with a few spots of blue (indicating scores above grade level), lots of green (on grade level), some yellow (progressing toward grade level), and some red (significant needs). We move through the data student by student discussing which students need further assessments to better understand their learning strengths and instructional needs.

My gut tightens as the group analyzes the data from one class to the next. I know what is coming, so I don't know why I have an emotional reaction, but I do. I've only been these students' teacher for a few weeks, and I already know they are significantly behind. Then, the data for my class flashes on the screen. The red stands out like a fire truck on the highway. I search for the spots of blue, yellow, and green. They are there, but these colors melt into the background as the red overwhelms the space.

Now the silence in the room is deafening. After a few moments, the curriculum coordinator kindly says, "Tam, your data looks a bit different from the other classrooms. We will make sure your class receives support from the reading specialist." I am grateful for the support, but my worries run deep at this moment. There is just so much red on the screen.

That night, I vented all of my worries to my husband for way longer, I am sure, than he wanted to hear. But that next morning, as I drove to work,

I thought about why I returned to the classroom after being a staff developer for over twenty years. It was at this moment that I made three promises to myself and the students in my classroom:

1. The student data will look drastically different in the spring.
2. My students will make reading growth joyfully, and we will celebrate every step of the way.
3. The stress of this data will reside within me and not within these kids.

This book is about the lessons I learned as I taught, assessed, taught, revised my thinking, taught, reassessed, and taught some more. It is the story of one class's journey, and how this class helped me revise my teaching practices. I wouldn't say that my practices changed in dramatic ways. Instead, this book is all about the small instructional moves that impacted students' literacy learning. And when these quick and frequent moves became part of my daily and weekly instructional routines, I saw students internalize skills, apply newly learned strategies, and build their confidence. Learners grew exponentially, and many moved from an "at-risk" status on multiple literacy screeners to grade-level readers by the end of the school year.

In each chapter of this book, I'll share snippets from the classroom so that you can get to know a few students. You will meet Jory, a second grader with a keen sense for numbers and a generous heart. Then, there is Maya. She loves to sing, and dance, and can often be found making handmade gifts for her classmates. Another student I will introduce to you is Sam. He is a fast-talking, fast-moving student who has bold opinions and loves to share them. He can often be found right in the middle of any situation. From leading games on the playground to organizing new projects in the classroom, or resolving a classroom conflict, Sam is at the center. To protect students' privacy, I've changed their names and altered many identifying details about them. At the same time, I tried to preserve and accurately depict their enduring spirits and capture the details of their learning journeys.

What these three students have in common is that they are all striving readers. The beginning of the year testing results from both the DIBELS and Fountas & Pinnell Benchmark Assessment System show that these readers need additional support to reach grade-level benchmarks. All of their scores on the beginning of the year spreadsheet are all fire-engine red.

In each chapter, I'll weave in stories about these students to illustrate ways quick and frequent instruction helped them make more than one year's growth in a year. But the quick and frequent moves I highlight will be about much more than just improving test scores. We'll look at quick and frequent practices that can give children the skills they need while also supporting them to build joyful reading lives for themselves. These students, like all learners, need opportunities to develop readerly identities with interests, tastes, and preferences. They, like all learners, need to feel like smart and capable people who can set, work toward, and achieve their goals. They, like all learners, can take the lead, teach others, and showcase their understandings through literary leadership moments.

This book is all about finding ways to make quick and frequent practice positive and empowering so that all students find their voice in their learning journey—a journey that will have ups and downs and many moments of both hard work and joy. Along the way, students will learn what it means to practice, so they can develop their own regimens and routines when they want to learn something new. They will also learn ways to celebrate their progress along the way and take opportunities to share their journey and accomplishments with others. These moments will allow them to reflect, recharge, and set forth again.

The stories I tell in this book are from my own second-grade classroom, and I hope they help you imagine what these teaching practices might look like in spaces in which you teach. I'll share stories of success, certainly, but in hopes of saving you time, I'll also share stories of my missteps, so you don't make the same mistakes I made. This way, you can make your own mistakes, and learn from them too.

Now, of course, these instructional moves aren't ones I invented alone. My teaching stands on the shoulders of the hundreds of teachers with whom I have collaborated over the last twenty years and the colleagues with whom I teach every day. These small moves are simply my interpretation of teaching practices I have learned and tried for years.

If you hope to read a book with fancy ideas, this is probably the wrong book for you. Instead, you will see my continued efforts to keep the materials simple and the prep minimal. The materials I use will be tools the students use regularly as they read and write. I do this intentionally so that students know how to use these tools when they work on their own, and I spend most of my prep time thinking about the next steps for my students and finding just the right books to make learning engaging and personal to them. I want to have choices of books that connect to students' interests and stretch them as readers, and I want to leave space for them to take the lead, share their insights, and coach others.

✔ How This Book Is Organized

I have organized this book in the way I plan my instruction each week. I start with student data and move to individualized and small-group instruction. Then I think about quick and frequent whole-class experiences to promote fluency, accuracy, comprehension, thinking, listening, speaking, perspective-taking, and self-reflection. Finally, I'll highlight ways to collaborate with families. Supporting learners isn't a task we can do alone, so throughout the book, I'll show how I share quick and frequent instructional practices with everyone who supports the students so that we all work on the same instructional goals to help them make accelerated growth.

In Chapter 1, we will take a deeper dive into student data. Through a case study of three students, you will see ways to build on student strengths and identify some potential first instructional steps. I'll share how I collect data as I teach and how I analyze the data to develop a weekly plan for small-group and individualized quick and frequent instruction. Most importantly, I'll show how I create this weekly plan in one planning period and how I keep it manageable to complete the plans I make each week. This chapter will not feel like a small move at all, and that is because it is not. This chapter is the foundational work I do so that my quick and frequent instruction is responsive to my students' needs, passions, and interests.

Chapter 2 is all about the small move I call, "Quick and Frequent Phonics Practice." This chapter is about the quick and frequent phonics instruction I plan to help kids become automatic with isolated foundational skills that they need to read and write fluently. I'll share what my quick and frequent instruction looks like, what materials I use, and how I fit it into an already busy day. These are also the plans I share with any individual who works in my classroom—whether they are there on a regular basis or a volunteer for one session. When there is an adult who has time, I want them to know exactly what to do and have the materials they need at their fingertips.

In Chapter 3, we will explore how quick and frequent instruction moves beyond phonics instruction and into building reading fluency. By using songs, poems, and Reader's Theater for repeated readings, students joyfully practice without realizing they are actually building fluency skills. Although most of this work happens during transitions, morning meetings, and a ten-minute block after recess, this quick and frequent practice becomes a playful part of learning. Through this work, students engage with grade-level texts that help them learn new vocabulary, internalize many high-frequency words, and infer deeper ideas about the meanings of a text. This work takes only a few minutes each day, but it is a linchpin that builds community, confidence, and stamina.

In the classroom, quick and frequent practice isn't solely about reading accurately and fluently. Yes, accuracy and fluency are essential, but alongside it, children need to construct meaning as they read and develop thought-provoking ideas. Throughout Chapter 4, we will look at ways to use quick and frequent practice to lift student voices, deepen how students think about texts, listen to other's perspectives, and express their thinking. These practices only take five to ten minutes a day, and they help children develop the skills they need to comprehend deeply.

When students meet people within their community and outside it, they learn stories of determination and perseverance. Understanding these people's learning journeys can help students both understand the purpose of quick and frequent instruction and ultimately know when and how to create learning paths for themselves. Chapter 5 is all about introducing students to people who have used quick and frequent moves to accomplish their goals over time. As these mentors illustrate, no matter what you want to accomplish in this world, practice is a part of the journey—it is a way we build stamina. Whether we need to overcome an obstacle, pursue a passion, or stand up for our rights or the rights of others, learning about how other people make small moves day after day to chip away at a problem or accomplish a goal helps us know what is possible. Through this work, students internalize the mantra "we can do hard things," develop their own goals, and know ways to reach them.

Kids are not just recipients of teachers' quick and frequent instruction. They need opportunities to plan quick and frequent instruction for themselves and others. Chapter 6 is all about making space for children to reflect on their learning, plan the next steps, and develop their own practice systems. Through this small move, we shift the teacher role to the students, and allow them to teach themselves and others. Our kids need practice taking the lead, developing plans, experiencing setbacks, and trying again. When we put our students in leadership positions, they learn to design quick and frequent steps for themselves, whenever they want to pursue a passion or overcome an obstacle.

As students learn more about how practice impacts learning, they also learn what determination and perseverance actually look, feel, and sound like. This way, no matter what they want to pursue after they leave our classrooms, they know that quick and frequent practice is a friend. It is a way we put one foot before the other to learn, grow, and change. Examples of these moments are highlighted throughout this book and labeled as "literacy leadership moments." Literacy leadership moments can be the fuel to propel kids forward.

We all know that our moments with our students are fleeting. We have 180 days of a child's life, and if we want to have deeper impacts, we must strengthen our collaborations with the people in students' lives. Chapter 7 focuses on quick and frequent ways to communicate and collaborate with the grown-ups in our students' homes. Here I'll talk about how students can make short videos to share their learning with their families, and how I create weekly videos that are under two minutes to provide families with a menu of ways to support their child's learning goals at home. In this chapter, you will

hear all about my mistakes and what I did when my initial attempts at communication failed. Through these failures, I learned some quick and frequent ways to create connections between home and school.

This book is really about teaching our kids the power of chipping away at something meaningful through quick and frequent practice. Throughout this book, I will show how I use quick and frequent moves to help students make significant gains, but more importantly how to actively involve them in the learning journey. I want students to see how short bursts of practice help them achieve their goals. I want them to understand that so many people around them who they admire have done just that—they have practiced. Most importantly, I want students to know that sometimes practice is joyful, and sometimes practice is arduous—but regardless, practice helps people achieve their goals, and even achieve goals that they didn't know were possible. To me, this work in the classroom is essential, because when it is not embedded into our daily instruction, I worry that students internalize messages that learning will just come, or worse, think that they do not have the capacity to learn a difficult concept or skill.

Thanks for joining me. As you read, please remember this is the story of the journey of one classroom in one school. Schools are all so different, and we have access to different resources, amounts of time to teach, numbers of students in class, and support personnel. As I share, I hope these ideas inspire you to identify quick and frequent moves that can have big impacts for your students.

I hope this book gives you some tips and ideas to enhance your instruction, strengthen collaborations, and give your students the agency to make their own learning plans and celebrate their successes throughout their journey. Like all of you, my teaching continues to evolve and grow each year. I hope that by sharing ideas and reflections, I'll inspire you to unlearn and relearn alongside me. Perhaps you can even share your ideas with me online. You know, we are all better teachers because we have each other.

Whether you are starting your thirty-fifth year or your first year, I wish you the most joyful teaching journey. No matter how busy some days are in the classroom, I know our work is filled with purpose, and this purpose keeps us coming back day after day.

Let's get started.

Happy Reading and Happy Teaching!

Tammy

1

Planning Quick and Frequent Moves

I sit next to Jory as she reads a new series for the first time. This book has more text on the page than she has ever read before. As Jory reads, I watch. I want to see how she applies her phonics skills and reading strategies independently. Her reading is slow at first, and I have to bite my lip a few times as she problem-solves some tricky words. But, after a few pages, she gets her stride and makes many deliberate moves as a reader.

After a few minutes, I stop her. "What did you notice about yourself as a reader?"

She shrugs, but I also see a smile hiding in that shoulder shrug.

"Can I tell you all the things I noticed about you as a reader?" I ask.

She nods reluctantly.

"Jory, look at my messy notes." I move my notebook in front of her so she can look at it as I talk. "Let me show you what they say. Look here. Do you remember when you got to this word *forget*? You put your fingers right in the book and found the two parts. Wow!"

Her chin lifts a bit.

"Can we look at another part? Do you see right here? First, you said *waved*, but then you looked closer and said all the parts and read *water*."

Jory responds this time, "I knew that *waved* didn't match."

"So now what are you thinking about yourself as a reader?"

"Well, there were a lot of words on those pages," she admits.

"I agree, and I hope you noticed your problem-solving. Please keep problem-solving as you read. I can see how it is working for you. I also can't wait for you to read more and tell me what you think of this new series. Thanks for reading with me."

I leave Jory's side, and her attention goes right back to the book.

As I work with Jory, I write a few notes, just as I try to do with every student I work with, even though it doesn't always happen. Over the course of a school day, my data collection is far from perfect. My notes are messy, and sometimes I forget to take them. There are moments when I record lots of information and others that slip away from me. What is most important is that I'll keep persisting to collect data as I teach without letting it overwhelm me or intrude on my moments with the kids. I'll keep trying because my notes matter. They help me think about the next possible teaching points with different students, new ideas for how to teach a concept, and which texts to put in the readers' hands.

TEACHER TIP

My notes also help my students. They help them see their growth, know what they are working on, and recognize what they are already doing so well. As the school year progresses and we have more conversations about students' learning processes, students will become more proficient at reflecting on the strategies they use and their progress, but for now, my notes are a big part of this reflection process. My students need my notes, and I need them too.

As I struggle with how to balance note-taking with the busyness of teaching, I keep John Hattie's words in my mind:

> There is no recipe, no professional development set of worksheets, no new teaching method, and no band-aid remedy. It is a way of thinking: "My role, as a teacher, is to evaluate the effect I have on my students." It is to "know thy impact," it is to understand this impact, and it is to act on this knowing and understanding. It requires that teachers gather defensible and dependable evidence from many sources, and hold collaborative discussions with colleagues and students about this evidence, thus making the effect of their teaching visible to themselves and others.

(2012, 19)

I know that if I am going to "know thy impact," I need to teach, watch, listen, and teach again. And I can't accomplish this goal from the front of the classroom. I need to spend lots of time working alongside students one-on-one and in small groups, and I need to record what I notice. The more I see what kids do as they read and write, the more specific my teaching becomes and the better I listen as kids talk about what they noticed about themselves as learners.

✔ Creating a Plan for Quick and Frequent Practice

Throughout this chapter, I'll share the messiness of my process and my attempts to find a manageable system to collect data and then use it to plan for individualized and small-group instruction for the following week. This plan is the linchpin in my teaching, and I don't start a week of instruction without it. To me, this plan is my brain on paper, and without it, I get caught up in the busyness of the school day and miss teaching opportunities. This system allows me to be ready to make the many quick and frequent moves I'll describe in this book. The quick and frequent moves are possible because I have a system that helps me listen to what my students say and watch what they do.

To give you a closer look at my process, I will show this plan using the data from three students: Jory, Maya, and Sam. You already met Jory at the beginning of this chapter, and you will get to know Sam and Maya in Chapter 2. I'll bring these students' stories to life in the first parts of this book so that when you look at my small-group plan, you can connect stories about these children to the instructional plans.

Now, of course, there are many more students in my class who need intensive instruction to become fluent and avid readers, but throughout this book, I will intentionally focus on these three students so that you can get to know them beyond their scores on a spreadsheet. I want you to know the children's stories behind the data so you can see ways to design quick and frequent moves around the students as whole people—their interests, learning needs, and work habits. Knowing the learners is the part of the assessment and instruction process that matters most. Instead of seeing spreadsheets of numbers, I hope these snippets about the children help you picture these three vibrant people in your mind. Perhaps Jory, Sam, and Maya will remind you of students you know in your own schools.

Now let's take a look at a sample weekly small-group and individualized instructional plan focused on Jory, Sam, and Maya. There are two parts to the plan.

1) Quick and Frequent Plan for Individualized Instruction

On this planning document [Figure 1.1], I list only the names of students who read below grade level and need extra practice with specific skills. This document is titled "Quick and Frequent Plan" because the instruction listed happens in two- to five-minute bursts throughout the day. I generally list instructional practice goals for six to eight students on this single-page document. Some students are listed every week, and others move in and out, depending on student needs.

The skills listed are ones that specific students need repeated practice with so they can apply this knowledge when reading and writing independently. I

Quick and Frequent Plan Week of January 9–13

NAMES	FOCUS
Sam Monday ___ Tuesday ___ Wednesday ___ Thursday ___ Friday ___	**Reading** Review two sounds of each vowel—use the chart in the mini sound book Read: were, our, want, word, write, called Read a chapter in the silent e decodable book **Writing:** Dictation: kit/kite, cap/cape, pet/Pete, hop/hope,
Jory Monday ___ Tuesday ___ Wednesday ___ Thursday ___ Friday ___	**Reading** Read: what, after, now, want Read a chapter in the blends decodable book Read: strong, cluck, mask, mend, slant **Writing:** Dictation: desk, mask, pond, skunk, last
Maya Monday ___ Tuesday ___ Wednesday ___ Thursday ___ Friday ___	**Reading:** Practice short vowel sounds i and u—use the chart in the mini sound book Read digraph word cards Read *Jack at Bat* **Writing:** Dictation: chop, chip, chap, check, much

Figure 1.1

A sample Quick and Frequent Plan for individualized instruction. See Appendix A for a blank copy of this planning form.

have taught some of these skills during whole-class and small-group lessons, and some students need more time and repetition for it to become automatic. Frequently, the skills in this plan were taught in previous grades, but these students do not know them yet. The skills listed on this planning sheet are ones that students need to practice until they have mastered them—meaning they know the skill so well they can apply it in new contexts automatically.

TEACHER TIP

Generally, the skills I list in the Quick and Frequent Plan are concepts I have previously taught, and which students need more practice to internalize. However, there are times when I use quick and frequent moves to pre-teach a concept so that the student will be more successful during whole-class lessons. Although this book will not focus on this type of quick and frequent practice, I think pre-teaching can be a helpful way to help children be successful in upcoming lessons.

When considering which concepts or skills to choose for these Quick and Frequent Plans, I carefully narrow down the list of tasks to what can be accomplished during a week's worth of practice. The goal is for these skills to become automatic, and that can't happen if there are too many. Remember, these quick and frequent sessions happen daily in two- to five-minute instructional moments throughout the school day. This work is in addition to my instruction during the literacy block, so the focus has to be narrow, and the tasks are skill-based and quick.

For me, reasonable means some of the following. Yes, the word "some" in the prior sentence is a crucial point. I typically choose two to three concepts from the following list:

- One or two phonemic awareness concepts (e.g., isolating, deleting, or manipulating phonemes).

- Reading or writing four to five letter sounds or letter sound combinations (e.g., short vowel sounds for a, i, and o, or the digraphs sh, ch, wh, and th).

- Reading or writing four to five words that follow a specific phonetic pattern (e.g., stack, stick, stock, stuck).

- Reading or writing four to five high-frequency words (e.g., the, am, said, and my).

- Reading a page or two from a text to help a student practice a specific skill.

- Adding a sentence to a writing piece the student is creating.

Before I write any skill next to a student's name, I ask myself two questions. (When I first started creating this document, I kept a sticky note with these questions on my computer to help me remember.)

1. Will this practice session give this student a skill they need when they read and write?
2. Can a student complete this practice with a teacher in two to five minutes?

If my answer is yes to both of these questions, then the skill goes on the sheet. If not, I revise my plan. These questions keep the practice sessions focused and manageable. For me, it is all about keeping it simple.

Once I have created the plan, I share it with the multiple teachers who come in and out of my classroom—English language learner (ELL) teachers, reading specialists, special education teachers, instructional assistants, and tutors. I email the weekly plan to them so they have it electronically, and I place a hard copy on a "teacher table" outside my classroom so anyone who provides instruction can access it. These teachers integrate the focus skills into their instruction so that the amount of practice a student receives daily is doubled and even tripled.

2) Quick and Frequent Plan for Small-Group Instruction

The second part of the Quick and Frequent Plan lists the small groups I will teach for the week. While only some students receive the individualized instruction from the first part of the Quick and Frequent Plan, all students work with me in small groups. On this small-group document, I list the groups of students I will meet with, what I will teach them, and when I will meet with each group. The concepts listed may appear less specific to an outside reader, but that is because this part of the weekly plan is just for me. Often, the instruction listed in this document is focused on helping children learn how to apply foundational skills as they read and write.

You will also notice that I list the times and days of the week when I will teach these groups and that some groups meet more frequently than others. This is intentional since some students need additional time and instruction to meet grade-level benchmarks. When I force myself to list the days and times of each small group, it is easier to implement these plans. Don't get me wrong, classroom life is super busy, and I don't always accomplish everything listed, but it keeps me focused and helps me remember what I thought was most important when I had moments to think.

Small-Group Plan Week of January 9–13

SMALL-GROUP INSTRUCTION	FOCUS
Reading	
Jory, Maya, and two other students, 10:00–10:15 (M, W, F)	Look through the whole word—watch for blends and digraphs
Sam and two students, 10:15–10:30 (M, W, F)	Look carefully for silent e
Four students, 10:00–10:15 (T, Th)	Create mind movies as you read
Six students, 10:30–10:45 (T, Th)	Reading punctuation
Assess: three students, 10:45–11:00 (T, W, F)	Phonics assessment
Writing	
Four students, 11:10–11:25 (M, W)	Generate topic ideas
Jory, Maya, Sam, and one student, 11:10–11:25 (T, Th)	Writing all the sounds you hear
Six students, 11:25–11:40 (M, W)	Elaborate—using small actions and dialogue
Four students, 11:25–11:40 (T, Th)	Dictation: ew, au, aw, oi, oy
Eight students, 11:10–11:50 (F)	Writing conferences
Quick and Frequent, 11:40–11:50 (M–TH)	

Figure 1.2
A sample small-group plan. (Usually, this document lists all students' individual names, rather than the number of students in the group. Student names have been removed in this example for privacy.) A blank copy of this planning form can be found in Appendix B.

What Happens in Small-Group Instruction

While the focus of small-group instruction is responsive to the readers I meet with, here are a few examples of what the small-group instruction (outlined in Figure 1.2) looks and sounds like.

SMALL-GROUP EXAMPLE #1

Focus Skill

Look Through the Whole Word—Watch for Blends and Digraphs

Warm-Up

"Let's practice the sounds of the digraphs so you know them so well you can use them to read and write words." Students open their mini sound books [Figure 2.3] and I say, "Say the word 'shut.' Tell your elbow partner what sound is at the beginning of the word 'shut.'" Students say and point to the digraph that spells sh. I repeat this exercise for each of the digraphs, choosing words that have digraphs at the beginning or ends of them.

Teaching

"Wow! Did you notice how well you know the sounds of ch, th, wh, and sh? Now let's practice how to use these as we read to help us solve unfamiliar words. Let's say I was reading along and I came to this word" (I write the word *bath* on the whiteboard).

"Tell your elbow partner what you know about this word and how you might solve it." I pause a moment for the students to discuss.

"That's right, when readers solve words they look for what they know, and then blend the parts together. You just used a digraph and the sounds of the other letters to solve a word."

Depending on the students' skills, I will repeat this work with three or four words, adding more complex words with digraphs at the beginning or end and with different short vowel sounds.

"Now let's try it in a book," I continue. I jot short sentences on the whiteboard from a familiar text that contains a word with a digraph. "Here are a few sentences right out of Jory's book." I point to (but don't read aloud) the sentences I have written—"Lots of dogs run past. Thin dogs, thick dogs. Tan dogs, black dogs."

"Read this sentence with your elbow partner and use what you know about the letters and sounds to solve new words."

Practice: Partner or Independent Reading

Depending on the students' level of independence with the focus skill, they either partner read or independently read a book that will support them to practice this skill. As the students work, I confer with several readers and take a few notes about possible next steps. Then, this group of students continues to read and I head off to my next small group.

SMALL-GROUP EXAMPLE #2

Focus Skill

Create Mind Movies as You Read

Warm-Up

I grab our class read-aloud, *Little Shaq* by Shaquille O'Neal, and turn to the next chapter. "Readers, I'm going to read just two sentences to you and I want you to act out what the character is doing as I read."

As the students act out in their seats, I remark, "Yes—you really understood what Little Shaq is doing in this part of the story. Now I'll read the next paragraph, but this time, instead of acting it out, picture what Little Shaq is doing in your mind and tell your elbow partner what you saw in your mind. You might say, 'I saw Little Shaq…'"

Teaching

"Readers, when you picture what is happening in a story in your brain, that is called making a mind movie. You are using your mind to make the characters move and talk in your head, just like you are watching a movie. Readers do this so that they understand and enjoy what they read."

Practice: Partner or Independent Reading

"Let's practice. Please take out the book you are reading from your book box. As you read, picture what is happening inside your head." As the students work, I confer with several readers and ask them to share what they see in their minds as they read. Then, I head off to another group or call the class together to wrap up reading time.

SMALL-GROUP EXAMPLE #3

Focus Skill

Reading Punctuation

Warm Up

"Readers, please tell your elbow partners, what is punctuation, and how does a reader use it?"

Teaching

Responding to what students say, I state my teaching point and write punctuation marks on the whiteboard. "Yes, readers. Punctuation marks are the commas, periods, question marks, exclamation points, and quotation marks writers use to help the reader know *how* to read the text. When readers pay attention to the punctuation and the words, they can bring the book to life. You read it just like you are talking, and that helps you understand what you read."

I hand out copies of one of the class's Reader's Theater scripts (refer to Quick and Frequent Fluency Moves in Chapter 3 for a list of resources). "Before you read what the first character says, take a look at the punctuation and tell your elbow partner what you notice." As the kids talk, I listen and then teach based off of what they say.

I might say something like, "That's right. These quotation marks tell us that a character is speaking, and the exclamation point at the end of the sentence tells us the character has a big feeling. Read that sentence with your elbow partner a few times and say the sentence aloud to bring out the character's big feelings. Remember to scoop words together so your reading sounds like talking."

Practice: Partner or Independent Reading

"Now let's try it with your Reader's Theater script. Please take your script out of your book box and read it. Remember to look closely at the words and the punctuation and make your voice match what the punctuation is telling you to do."

As the students work, I confer with several readers, asking them to read aloud, and coaching them to improve their fluency. Then, I head off to another group or call the class together to wrap up reading time.

Ready to Go!

Now that I have my two-part Quick and Frequent Plan for the week, I have a bit of "brain space" as I teach. This plan is on my clipboard, so I don't have to think about what to teach or emphasize. Instead, I have more energy to give feedback in the moment, listen closely, record my observations, and ultimately "know thy impact." (Thanks, John Hattie.) My plan reminds me who, what, and when I will teach in each small group and lists the additional skill work I will complete with students who need extra support. A quick glance at these two pages jogs my memory so I can be more present with the kids.

When I first began to create this two-part plan, it took over an hour to complete. But now, I can create it during a planning period on Friday as long as I can sit quietly and am not exhausted from the week. If I am a bit tired, which happens more than I want to admit, I finish it over the weekend. I definitely *do not* plan when I am too tired to think. I use those times to organize the classroom and save small-group planning for when I can focus.

✔ Steps to Create the Weekly Quick and Frequent Plan

Let's take a closer look at the steps I take to create the weekly Quick and Frequent Plans.

Step 1: Collecting Data

Collecting data is all about choosing meaningful learning targets for students. This means that my note-taking needs to be strong. When it is weak, I can feel it when I plan.

I will warn you right now: my data-collection process might feel overwhelming to you, and that is okay. My system works for me, and that is what matters. I hope reading about my system inspires and supports you to create a system that works for you. Here are the questions I thought about to create my system:

- How can I collect data during whole-class, individual, and small-group instruction in a manageable way?

- How can I collect information from all the people who work with my students?

- Is there technology that is already collecting student data that I can review?

With these questions in mind, I created multiple ways to collect data.

1) Conferring Notebook

I take notes in a notebook. I place tabs (one per student) in that notebook, and when I work with students, I record what I see and think are the next steps.

As you can see in Figure 1.3, my notes are pretty messy. They generally consist of informal running records, observations I make about a child's reading disposition and notes about their understanding of the text. I also use this notebook to collect data as I formally assess. Whenever I administer any district-required assessments, I look over the data with this notebook in hand.

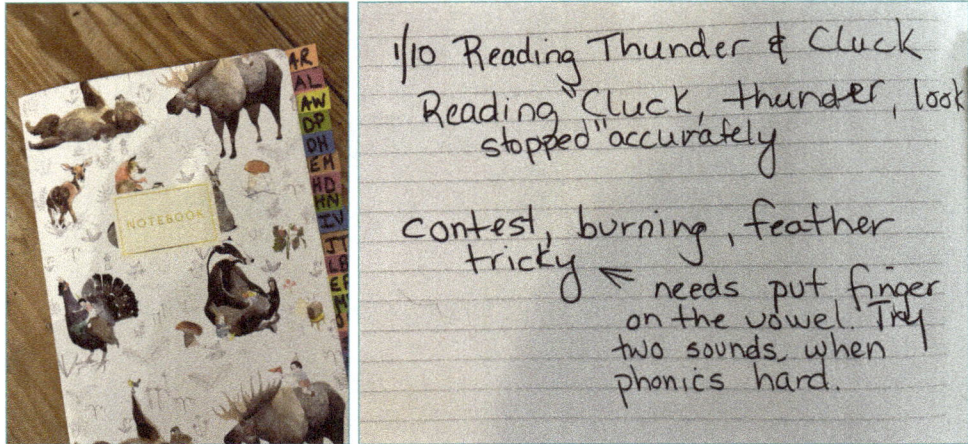

Figure 1.3
My notebook with a tab for each student (left) and an example of a note I took while listening to a student read (right).

This way all of my notes are in one place, and I take this notebook out each week when I construct my weekly plan.

Many people write notes in an Excel spreadsheet and carry a device as they teach. I've tried, and it just doesn't work for me. I like my pretty notebook and the organic nature of my notes. It is easy for me to carry around the classroom and put it in my bag to take home at the end of the day.

2) Excel Spreadsheet

While I prefer to record my notes in a notebook, I do create an Excel spreadsheet so that any teacher who works with one of my students can record their observations. This spreadsheet is very simple. I have a tab for each student who is listed on the weekly Quick and Frequent Plan, and each student's sheet in Excel has a three-column chart: Date/Learning Goal/Notes. Once I have the Quick and Frequent Plan completed for the week, I simply copy and paste the learning goals onto the Excel spreadsheet. This way, the other teachers who work in my room can record notes as they work with students.

Figure 1.4 shows a few days of notes on the Excel spreadsheet for Jory. At this point in the year, Jory needs additional practice to read high-frequency words automatically and remember her blends. The goals listed in Column B are simply copied from page one of the Quick and Frequent Plan for the week of 1/9. The teacher who worked with the student (i.e., instructional aide or another support teacher) recorded their observations in the third column.

I want to be clear: I do not write notes on this Excel spreadsheet. I write notes in my conferring notebook. The only information I add to this Excel spreadsheet each week is the weekly learning goals for the few students with individualized goals on the Quick and Frequent Plan. Now, the teachers who move in and out of my classroom record notes on those students. The Excel spreadsheet is there so I can learn from teachers who enter my room about what they notice when they work with students. At the end of the week, I will look at these notes and use this information in combination with my notes to plan the upcoming week's instruction. Here is a sample Excel spreadsheet for Jory. Notice that that the skills listed under focus match the skills listed on the Quick and Frequent plan on page 10.

DATE	FOCUS	NOTES
1/9	**Reading** Read: what, after, now, want Read a chapter in the decodable book. Read: strong, cluck, mask, mend, slant **Writing:** Dictation: desk, mask, pond, skunk, last	Needs to practice Slow on Tevin, Jazmin, Tevin, chips. Said them word by word
1/10	**Reading** Read: what, after, now, want Read a chapter in the decodable book. Read: strong, cluck, mask, mend, slant **Writing:** Dictation: desk, mask, pond, skunk, last	Confused what and want Got the names; reading words along and limps was hard Short u was hard. Tapped each sound carefully.
1/11	**Reading** Read: what, after, now, want Read a chapter in the decodable book. Read: strong, cluck, mask, mend, slant **Writing:** Dictation: desk, mask, pond, skunk, last	Got it smoother Said sounds but blended faster. Got short u. Wrote faster

Figure 1.4
This is the Excel spreadsheet where any support teacher who works in my room records their observations after working with a student. The goals listed in Column B match Jory's goals on the Quick and Frequent Plan. I create a different tab for each student who receives additional instruction from a support teacher.

3) Conferring Grid

Right on my clipboard, behind a copy of my Quick and Frequent Plans for the week, I keep a conferring grid like the one in Figure 1.5. This conferring grid is a two-sided one-page document that has two boxes for each student. In one box, I jot quick observations about literacy (L), and in the other box, I record observations during math (M). As I am teaching the whole class and notice something I want to remember about a student, I jot it down. During a phonics lesson, I might think, *Oh, Jory doesn't know the three sounds of -ed. She is writing a "t" instead of "ed" in words like "looked."* Or when I listen to students turn and talk during read-aloud, I might think, *Sam isn't sure what I mean when I say, "What is that character like?"* These notes can also be as simple as noticing that Maya needs more work with writing the letters b/d, as she is reversing those letters when she writes a dictated sentence.

I want to capture these observations the moment they happen because if I don't, I won't remember at the end of the day. So while the notes in my conferring grid may look like gibberish to others, I know what they mean. For me, it is all about capturing my observations so I can incorporate my thinking into next week's small-group and individualized plan. I find that when I write it down, I can relax more as I teach. The paper helps me know I won't forget these teaching points, so I don't have to teach *everything* right now. Instead, I can look over all of the possible teaching points and choose priorities. When I do this, I stay focused on specific goals rather than moving randomly between teaching points.

4) Computer-Based Data

In my classroom, students spend about fifteen minutes a few days a week during the beginning months of the year on Lexia—a computer-based reading program. This program provides online reports of student progress and flags skills that students need to learn. As I make a weekly plan, I look at these reports to give me another perspective. I compare these results with my own notes to determine learning goals. When I see areas where my students need direct instruction or additional practice, I add them to my Quick and Frequent Plan.

5) Seesaw Student Videos

About once a month, students create videos on Seesaw to demonstrate what they know. Depending on our whole-class literacy goals, students might show me how they solved a tricky word, what they noticed about the characters in their series

Math and Literacy   Week of :

JORY		MAYA		SAM	
L Short e and i Reading blends Three sounds of ed	M	L Short u and i b/d	M	L Silent e Character feelings	M
STUDENT NAME		STUDENT NAME		STUDENT NAME	
L	M	L	M	L	M
STUDENT NAME		STUDENT NAME		STUDENT NAME	
L	M	L	M	L	M
STUDENT NAME		STUDENT NAME		STUDENT NAME	
L	M	L	M	L	M
STUDENT NAME		STUDENT NAME		STUDENT NAME	
L	M	L	M	L	M
STUDENT NAME		STUDENT NAME		STUDENT NAME	
L	M	L	M	L	M
STUDENT NAME		STUDENT NAME		STUDENT NAME	
L	M	L	M	L	M

Figure 1.5
A conferring grid with space to write notes about students' math and literacy learning. See Appendix C for a blank copy of the conferring grid.

book, or give a retelling of a text they read independently. During writing time, they might read me what they wrote and explain what they tried to do as a writer.

I love that these videos let me peek into a student's thinking processes. After watching a student's video, I can leave a personal voice note where I share what they did well and something to continue to practice. Then once I approve the student's video, the family can see the Seesaw video and hear my voice note. This gives the folks at home a snapshot of what the child is working on, and they can hear a snippet of my teaching.

As I watch student videos, I have my conferring notebook in front of me. When I notice observations about a student, I jot them down. This way, I can incorporate these observations into my planning.

The bottom line is that it doesn't matter so much *where* I write the notes because what is most important is that I write them. Keeping my note-taking tools right near all the places I teach helps make sure that the note-taking happens. My conferring grid is on my clipboard that I keep by my side as I teach whole-class lessons. My conferring notebook generally stays at the table where I conduct small-group and individual conferences. This way, there is a place to record notes wherever I am in the classroom. Then, once a week, I can look at these notes together to create a Quick and Frequent Plan for the following week.

If note-taking and figuring out student learning goals are newer for you, you may want to take a look at the next section, "Teacher Resources I Use," and think about taking notes right on one of these tools. Sometimes having a list of possible teaching points on your note-taking sheet is helpful. Many teachers simply write student names next to specific learning goals as they teach. This system can be just as effective as the more open-ended one I use. The bottom line is to use what works for you. All you need to record is the student's name, what they are currently doing well, and some possible next steps. As we all know, there are limitless ways to do this, so try one system. If you are anything like me, you will change your system multiple times as you teach.

Teacher Resources I Use

List of Phonics Skills and Corresponding Words and Sentences

As I plan, I have a trajectory of phonics skills and lists of words right next to me. Since my school uses the phonics program Fundations, I keep the word lists from the end of each unit in one small folder. These pages give me access to quick lists of words and sentences for each phonetic concept and remind me of the order of the skills. Having lists of words and sentences that focus on one specific phonics skill saves lots of time. I don't need to self-generate these words or look them up. The words are right there, which makes it easy for students to read lists off the page, or I can use them for dictation. (Yes, my kids do read the words right off the teacher page, and they often comment that it is pretty cool to use the teacher manual!) See Chapter 6, Quick and Frequent Moves to Help Readers Lead, for more about giving kids teacher tools.

What to Teach by Level

Many resources list the skills students need to learn and different levels of text complexity. (I use "A Tool for Supporting Moving Readers Up Levels" (2021) from the Teachers College Reading and Writing Project to help me remember the skills students need to learn to read specific text levels.) A student who reads independently at a text complexity level of E needs very different phonics skills than someone reading level M. This is the document I pull out and put alongside my phonics data to help me think about what strategies students need to learn to apply their phonics skills as they read. It also helps me think about the fluency and comprehension goals I should focus on with students.

What I Will Teach the Whole Class

To know what to teach my whole class, I rely on the Massachusetts State Standards and the teaching points inside my district's curriculum to give me the big picture of what students need to learn. When I understand these concepts, I can foresee which skills will be tricky and require more whole-group support and which may be easier for students to apply independently.

Now all I have to do is put all of these resources together, and I have a plan.

Step 2: Putting the Notes Together

Before I plan the whole-class lessons for the upcoming week, I create a draft of my Quick and Frequent Plan. I do this because I want the students' learning goals and my observations to drive my instruction before I think about the whole-class lessons.

Sometimes my small-group notes will show me that I need to revisit a skill with the whole class because the majority of the students have not mastered it yet. This happened during our nonfiction reading unit of study. After listening to students retell and watching their videos on Seesaw, I realized that students really didn't understand how to categorize information into subtopics and details. This observation informed my whole-class lessons and helped me reteach this skill.

The reverse also happens. Sometimes I need to look at the upcoming whole-class lessons to determine the small-group teaching points. If the skill or strategy is tricky, I will teach the concept to the whole class, and then guide students through the new learning again in small groups. It all depends on what I am teaching, where I am in a particular unit of study, and what my students need.

Let's Look at the Process for One Student

Since you already know a bit about Jory, let's take a closer look at her assessment data and plan possible next steps together. Please remember that as you read my analysis, you may want to make decisions different from the ones I show. Two teachers might see different teaching points, and both paths will help the student grow. My hope is that this example helps you analyze the data you collect and make the best teaching decision you can.

Let's take a look at a snapshot of a partial running record I took when listening to Jory read *Muffin*—a Jump Rope Reader written by Sarah Mann and illustrated by Keenon Ferrell [Figure 1.6]. This text is a decodable book focused on words with short vowels, digraphs, and blends.

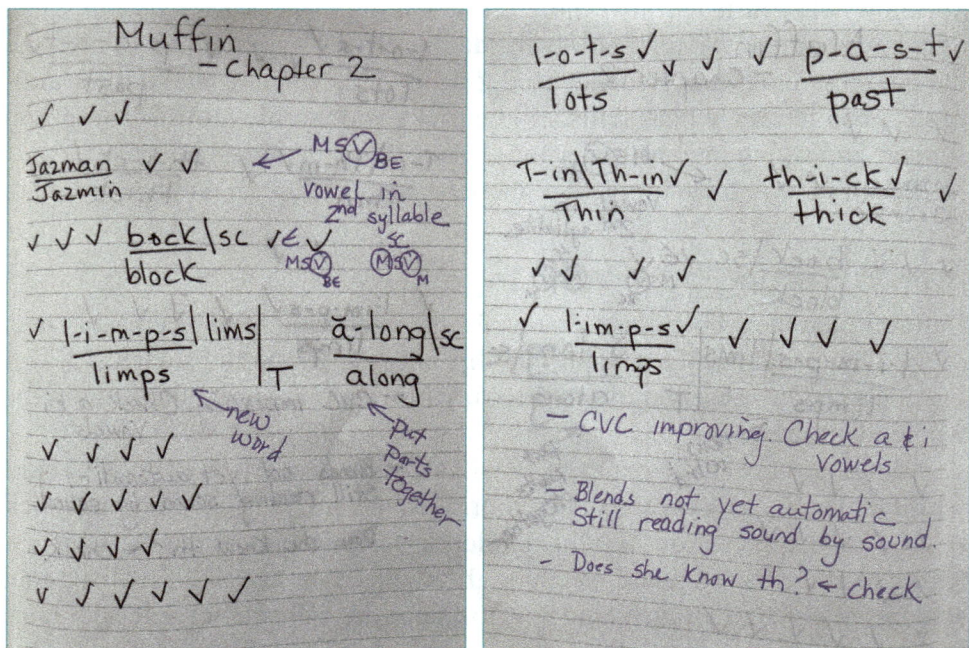

Figure 1.6
A partial running record and notes from Jory's reading of the decodable text *Muffin*.

I notice that, in this reading, Jory blends CVC words and reads some high-frequency words accurately. She reads *Dad*, *hip*, *kids*, and *pass* automatically. She also reads the high-frequency words *with*, *her*, *they*, *by*, and *into* correctly. When Jory reads an unfamiliar word (such as *limps*), she says the sounds in the word individually and then blends them. She is not reading the words with blends and digraphs automatically yet. However, the running record shows she is working hard on this skill as she reads.

After reading a few pages, Jory's body language confirms my thoughts. She leans back in her chair, stretches, and yawns. These behaviors are not a one-time occurrence, and I notice them whenever the task becomes difficult. All of this information shows me that Jory's efforts to decode require quite a bit of mental energy and her stamina wanes after reading a few pages. Does she need some other text choices that are more engaging and that she can read with a higher rate of accuracy? I decide to introduce her to the *Jack* series since she loves softball and dogs.

Later that week, Jory reads *Jack at Bat* written by Mac Barnett and illustrated by Greg Pizzoli. Figure 1.7 shows my conference notes:

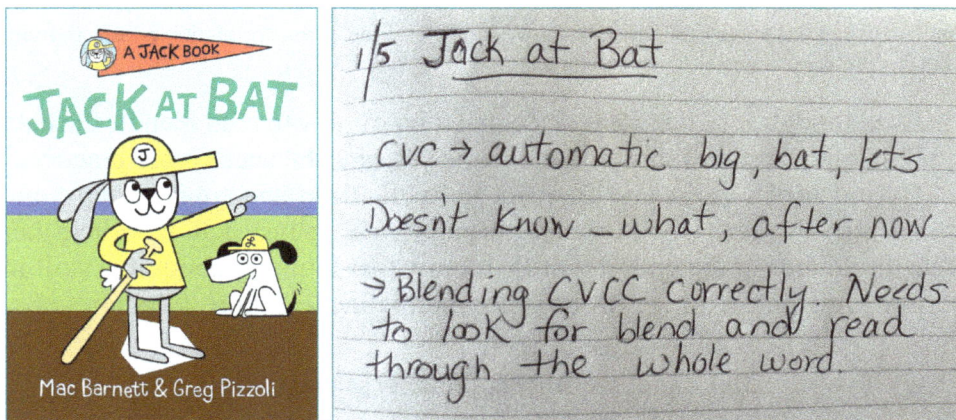

Figure 1.7
Conference notes from Jory's reading of *Jack at Bat*

Jory automatically reads *big*, *bat*, *lets*, *picks*, as well as *game* and *day*. She knew the high-frequency words, *it*, *is*, *the*, *not*, and *for*, but needed support with *what*, *after*, and *now*.

When she came to the words *Brats*, *pitch*, *Rex*, and *left*, she said each sound and then blended the sounds together. This shows that she is working on these skills. As expected, Jory needs a teacher's support with words such as *ladies*, *town*, *and root* (two-syllables and vowel diphthongs are phonics concepts she does not know yet). However, *Jack at Bat* is a story about a topic Jory knows a lot about and loves and that helped her persevere.

Since Jory is so interested in softball, and loves that the *Jack* books are chapter books, she will reread *Jack at Bat* multiple times, and on subsequent rereads her automaticity and fluency will improve. Despite the slow reading, Jory retells what she reads accurately and can describe how the characters feel in different parts of the story.

Now let's look at some phonics data I recently collected: The data from the CORE Phonics Survey [Figure 1.8] confirms what I see. When reading CVCC words, Jory needs guided practice.

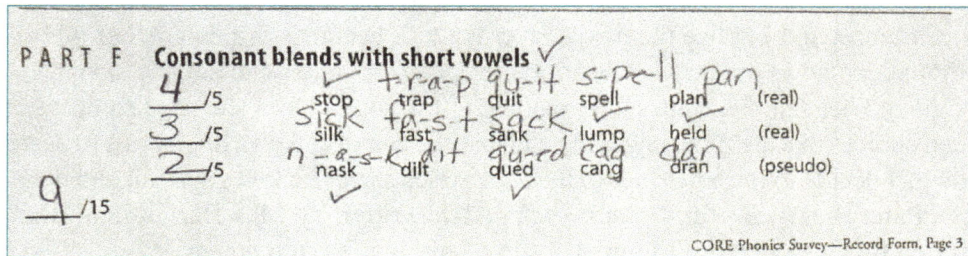

Figure 1.8
The CORE Phonics Survey confirms that Jory needs more work with consonant blends with short vowels. This assessment is available online (Burkins and Yates 2008).

Even though Jory has some understanding of how to read blends, the data is telling me that the skill is not automatic yet, and she needs more practice.

During Jory's quick and frequent individualized and small-group time, I also plan to teach about blends through writing instruction to help her hear the sounds at the end of words. I know that thinking about this skill in both reading and writing will help her internalize it. Figure 1.9 shows how

Quick and Frequent Plan Week of January 9–13

NAMES	FOCUS
Jory Monday ____Tuesday ____ Wednesday ____ Thursday ____ Friday ____	**Reading** Read: what, after, now, want Read a chapter in the blends decodable book. Read: strong, cluck, mask, mend, slant **Writing:** Dictation: desk, mask, pond, skunk, last

Figure 1.9
Both reading conference and formal phonics assessment data help guide Jory's Quick and Frequent individualized instruction.

I turned my observations into teaching priorities on the Quick and Frequent Plan. Notice the connections between what I observed about Jory and what I wrote in the plan?

Now take a look at the small-group page of my Quick and Frequent Plan [Figure 1.10] and notice the groups that Jory will participate in during the week. Here, you can see what strategies I decided to focus on and how they connect the skill work and strategic word solving.

Small Group Plan Week of January 9–13

SMALL-GROUP INSTRUCTION	FOCUS
Reading	
Jory, Maya, and two other students, 10:00–10:15 (M, W, F)	Look through the whole word—watch for blends and digraphs
Sam and two students, 10:15–10:30 (M, W, F)	Look carefully for silent e
Four students, 10:00–10:15 (T, Th)	Create mind movies as you read
Six students, 10:30–10:45 (T, Th)	Reading punctuation
Assess: Three students, 10:45–11:00 (T, W, F)	Phonics assesment
Writing	
Four students, 11:10–11:25 (M, W)	Generate topic ideas
Jory, Maya, Sam, and one student, 11:10–11:25 (T, Th)	Writing all the sounds you hear
Six students, 11:25–11:40 (M, W)	Elaborate using small actions and dialogue
Four students, 11:25–11:40 (T, Th)	Dictation: ew, au, aw, oi, oy
Eight students, 11:10 – 11:50 (F)	Writing conferences
Quick and Frequent, 11:40–11:50 (M–TH)	

Figure 1.10
A Quick and Frequent Plan for Small Groups

Now, I know what you are thinking—"But I have twenty-four (or more!) kids in my class, and I can't do this level of analysis for everyone." I agree, and I can't do it either. I do this level of analysis for readers who are not yet meeting grade-level benchmarks. Remember—the individualized instruction part of the Quick and Frequent Plan is only for students who need additional support. It is the small-group page that includes everyone.

At the beginning of the school year, when I first began creating these Quick and Frequent Plans, it took two hours to complete because I was starting from scratch. I didn't know my kids yet, and I didn't have a planning sheet that worked for me. Now that I know my students, I have a note-taking system and a format for planning individualized instruction and small groups, so the process is much easier. As the school year progresses, I revise the Quick and Frequent Plan each week, rather than creating from scratch. Sometimes kids' goals change from week to week, but often they don't change for a few weeks. I make sure that I stick with a goal until a child knows it automatically. Children need to know their phonics skills and high-frequency words so that they don't have to think about them. A phrase I often use in reference to these foundational skills is "it needs to be in a child's bones." These thoughts help me to stay focused on the same goals over a few weeks.

On the other hand, I also watch for when a skill is a mismatch for a child—it just doesn't seem like a reasonable entry point for them. It is in these moments that I need to change the focus and try an alternate skill. Teaching someone to read is both an art and a science. We must watch closely, collect these observations, and adjust so that all readers grow exponentially.

For me, this two-part weekly plan—quick and frequent individualized instruction for striving readers and small groups for everyone—keeps my teaching purposeful. All I know is that no matter how long this process takes or who the support personnel are in my room, I'll keep planning this way. After a few weeks or months, the planning pays off, and I can see the progress that the kids make. And isn't that why we are all teaching? It is one of the biggest joys of teaching when the young people in front of us grow and have ownership of their reading and writing lives.

2

Quick and Frequent Phonics Moves

It is Day 30 of the school year, and that feeling comes over me. I look into Maya and Sam's eyes during my whole-class phonics lesson. The class is learning to read and spell words with suffixes, -s, -es, -ed, -er, and -ing. As I watch them, I think, *You both need to learn this, but you really need to practice blending and segmenting single-syllable words with simpler phonetic concepts. Am I really doing what is best for you? Am I giving you exactly what you need in the moment you need it?*

The honest truth is no. These children need lessons much earlier in the phonics scope and sequence.

Now that teacher worry comes over me. You know the "teacher worry"— the one where you wake up at 3:15 a.m. figuring out how to "fix things" in your classroom. At first, I justify what I am doing, "My whole-class phonics lessons *do* have repeated practice," but the truth is, it is not enough for readers who need much more exposure. Sam, Jory, Maya, and a few other students need many repetitions to make learning stick, and they need to practice concepts that are further back on the phonics scope and sequence.

My middle-of-the-night thoughts flit from thinking about Maya's phonics knowledge to other moments with her. I remember the Monday morning when she arrived at school with her pockets filled with friendship bracelets she had created for everyone. She couldn't wait to show me all of them and pass them out to her classmates. Then there was the time she came running up to me right after she unpacked her school bag, "Mrs. Mulligan, Mrs. Mulligan, I think this note was supposed to go to my sister's teacher. The note says Rose's name and it is in my backpack." Then she dashed off to her sister's classroom to deliver the note.

These images leave me, and my mind flashes to a recent reading conference with Maya. As she read, she confused the short vowel sounds i and u and was unclear about when a vowel makes a long or short sound. She had a similar problem with the digraphs sh, and ch, often switching the sounds as she read.

Maya needs more practice with these specific skills until she becomes more automatic, and I need to change my instruction to support her. Figure 2.1 shows a snapshot of my conferring notes alongside results from the CORE Phonics Survey assessment.

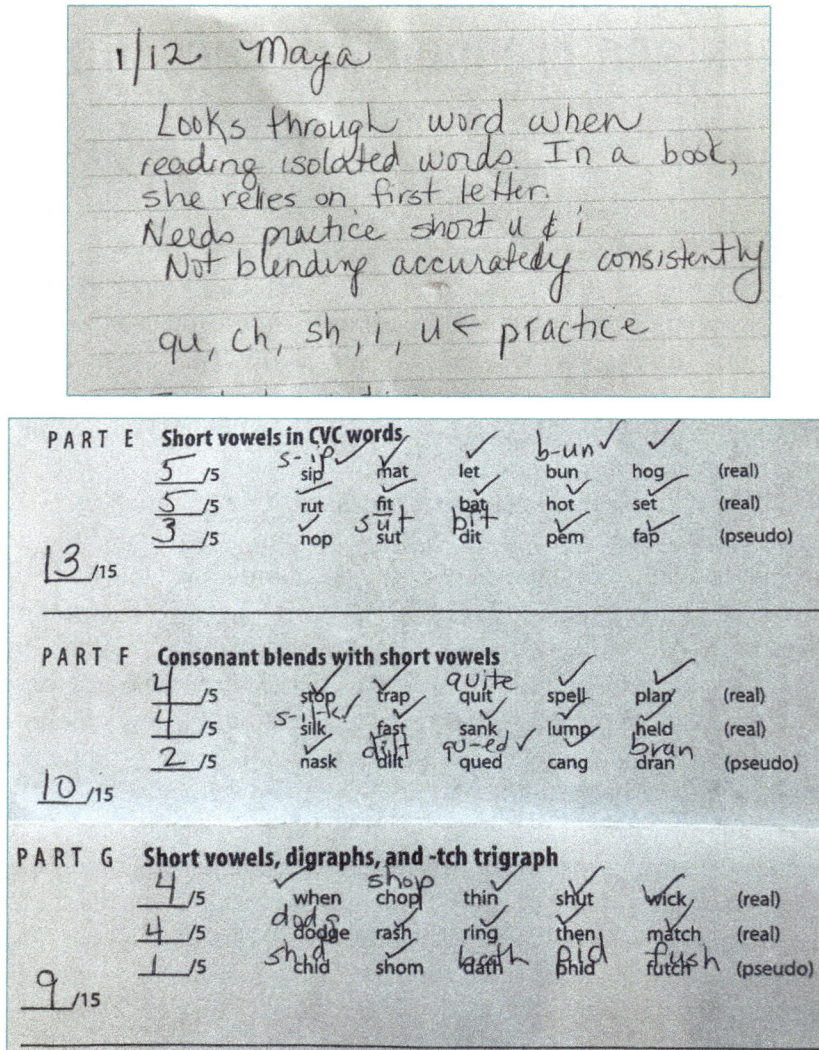

Figure 2.1
My conferring notes and CORE Phonics Survey assessment data on Maya.

Now that I've mentally planned for what Maya needs, even though it is 3:30 a.m., my mind jumps to Sam because my whole-group lesson isn't a perfect match for him either.

I see Sam in my mind as kids flock around him during indoor recess. Everyone is clamoring to get a spot at the table because Sam is teaching how to make a paper airplane. Then I see Sam by his cubby. Each day, he searches his backpack for the gadget he brought to school to show his peers.

Now I think back to a recent afternoon in our classroom. Sam is working alone at a table in the corner of the classroom. As I approach, he says, "Mrs. Mulligan, I am making a surprise for you. Don't come over yet." Later, I found a note on my laptop. It said: "I relly like school. I have frends here."

And now my mind once again returns to my phonics lesson worries.

As a reader, Sam reads CVC and CVCC words accurately and knows many first-grade high-frequency words (Sam is in second grade but is still learning to read some first-grade high-frequency words). However, when Sam encounters more complex phonics skills such as silent e or vowel teams, he is unsure, especially when he reads these words in isolation. Figure 2.2 shows a snapshot of Sam's assessment data.

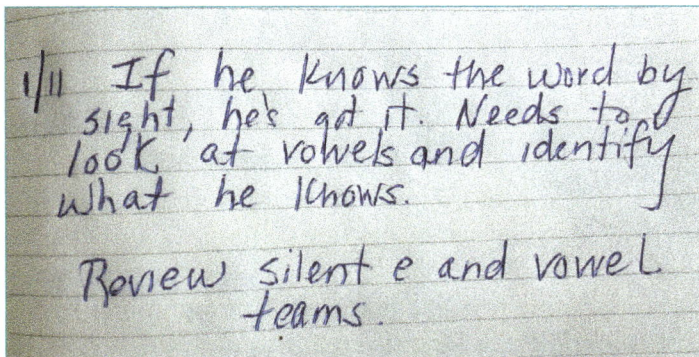

Figure 2.2
My conferring notes and CORE Phonics Survey assessment data on Sam.

With these two kids swirling in my head, I get out of bed and start reading my professional books . . . never a good idea at 3:45 a.m. I read Wiley Blevin's recommendations in *A Fresh Look at Phonics* in which he writes, "The bottom line is that it takes far more time for many students to master basic phonics skills than our curriculum allows. . . . The only way to ensure mastery then is to create a formal review and repetition cycle" (2016, 51). I stop and reread this section. The formal review and repetition cycles are missing from my instruction.

Now I've got some figuring out to do. I need to slide more practice sessions of previous skills into an already busy school day, and there are no "extra" blocks of time. So instead, I think about two five-minute practice sessions. This idea feels manageable to me, but more importantly, I think it will feel manageable to the kids. I think about tasks I would rather not do—washing dishes, folding laundry, cleaning the bathroom. One thing that makes them so arduous for me is how monotonous they become. But if someone told me, "Please wash dishes for two minutes. Don't worry about finishing all of them; just get a couple done," that would feel pretty doable. Now, if I did dishes for two minutes twice a day for several days in a row, I bet I would be surprised at how many dishes got washed. In fact, more likely than not, the dishes would be done by the end of a few days. Even if the dishes aren't completely finished, at least the pile is much smaller.

Right now, in some learners' lives, these rote skills are a little bit like washing dirty dishes. As I write that last sentence, I wish it wasn't true. I wish all aspects of learning to read and write were completely joyful. But there are times in learning when certain skills need to become automatic and the amount of practice to attain automaticity can feel daunting. Learners need lots of repetitive practice that uses different modalities—speaking, listening, and manipulating sounds; reading and writing isolated words; and reading and writing authentically. The Quick and Frequent Plan for Individualized Instruction (introduced in Chapter 1) is all about repeated practice, and the brain research tells us that repeated practice helps make learning stick.

Regina G. Richards in her article "Making It Stick: Memorable Strategies to Enhance Learning" writes, "Repetition and rehearsal of information enhance a process called consolidation, the process by which memories are moved from temporary storage in the hippocampus (a small structure within the brain) to more permanent storage in the cortex (the outer layer of the brain) (Richards, 2003, p. 24)" (2024). So in my classroom, two- to five-minute quick and frequent sessions for the students who need it become another small move with big impacts. These mini bursts of instruction help learners consolidate skills and keep learning joyful, purposeful, and quick.

In Chapter 1, I described how I use data to plan quick and frequent instruction for the children who need more intensive practice. This chapter is all about how to bring these plans to life in the classroom. Let's take a look at how I implement the weekly Quick and Frequent Plans, including ways to keep the materials manageable, find time in an already busy day, and optimize the many adults who come in and out of our classrooms.

✔ Materials with Multiple Uses

Forewarning: You should stop reading if you are looking for "Pinterest Worthy Materials." I have three personal rules about materials: (1) keep them super simple, (2) create materials that work even when learning goals change, and (3) make sure the students will use these materials to read and write throughout the school day and as their skills progress.

So before I create new materials or search the internet for something, I ask myself two questions:

1. What whole-class charts or experiences have we already used in class that could be used for additional practice?
2. What tools do the students already have and know how to use that could be used for additional practice?

I know that if I don't keep the materials very simple, the quick and frequent instructional times will fall by the wayside. There are too many things on a teacher's to-do list, and there isn't time to squeeze in one more piece of preparation. Our time is better spent collecting data as we teach and later analyzing those notes to plan instruction. Here are my very simple go-to materials.

Mini Sound Book with Keywords and Visuals

The kids use these mini sound books [Figure 2.3], which are about the size of my hand, during reading and writing workshops, whole-class phonics lessons, my small-group instruction, and individual practice sessions. These books are just mini versions of the charts from The Six Shifts website and our phonics

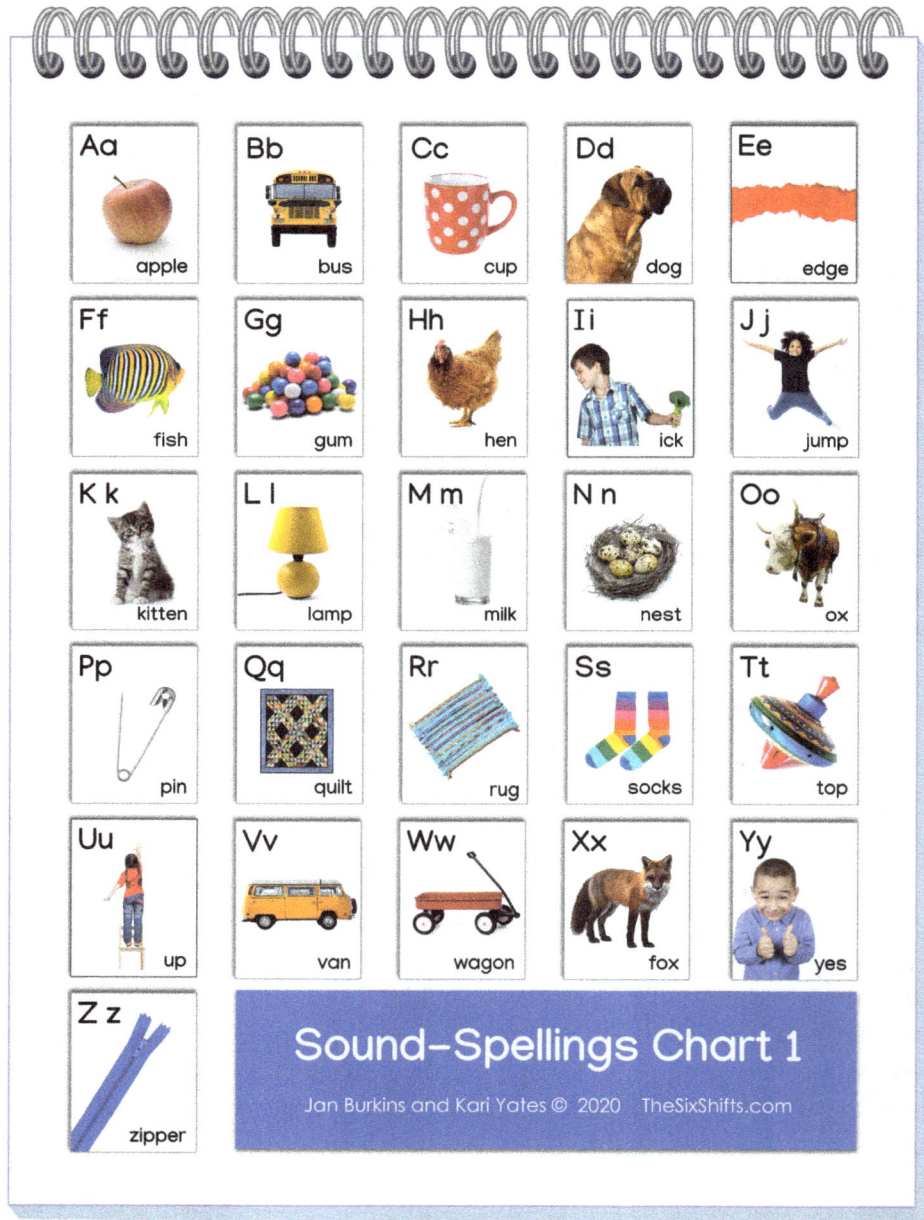

Aa apple	Bb bus	Cc cup	Dd dog	Ee edge
Ff fish	Gg gum	Hh hen	Ii ick	Jj jump
Kk kitten	Ll lamp	Mm milk	Nn nest	Oo ox
Pp pin	Qq quilt	Rr rug	Ss socks	Tt top
Uu up	Vv van	Ww wagon	Xx fox	Yy yes
Zz zipper				

Sound-Spellings Chart 1

Jan Burkins and Kari Yates © 2020   TheSixShifts.com

Figure 2.3
Using the Sound-Spellings Chart from Jan Burkins and Kari Yates, along with charts from my district's phonics program, I create mini sound books for my students. These mini sound books contain all the sound/letter combinations students will learn in grades K–2. Having these resources all in one place gives me options to review different sounds with different kids and even pre-teach new ones.

curriculum. The students are familiar with them because I have full-sized versions in the room as well. To make these mini sound books I put all the charts for the year in the order of the scope and sequence, laminate them, and bind them together.

TEACHER TIP

If you are looking for Sound-Spelling charts, check out the free downloads available from The Six Shifts website.

I know what you are thinking: "My kids are going to take that binding off in two seconds." I thought the same thing, but it only happened once. When the binding came off, I talked about it with the class, we problem-solved, and the situation was over. Most of the books last the entire school year and I can reuse them. I keep five of these mini sound books in my small-group teaching bin and the rest are out on student tables so both students and teachers can access them whenever kids are reading and writing.

Mini Composition Notebooks

Mini composition notebooks [Figure 2.4] are the place where students complete the quick and frequent practice listed on the weekly plan. When I want children to read five words with a specific phonetic concept, I write them on a page in their mini notebook. When students complete a dictation during a quick and frequent session, they write it in here. The size of this notebook is intentional—it gives a clear message that this practice won't take much time at all.

In the past, I used to use small strips of lined paper for a similar purpose. The small size helped kids, but what I didn't like about that system

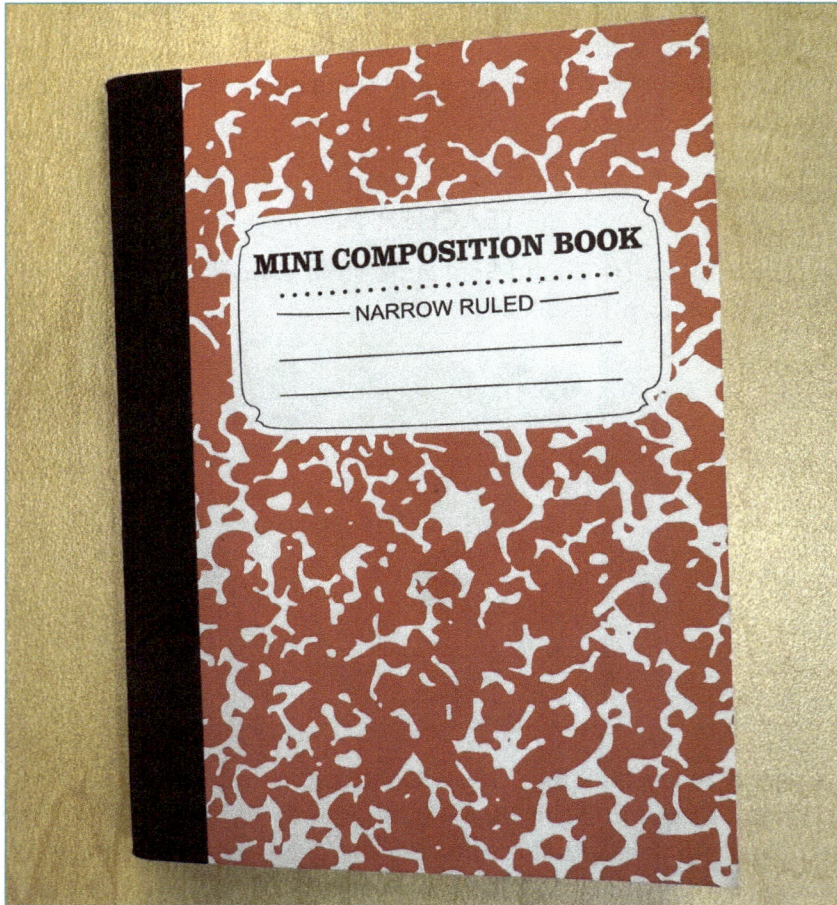

Figure 2.4
Mini composition notebooks (4.5″ by 3.25″) are a great space for quick and frequent practice.

was that when practice was over the paper went into the recycling bin. Now, with these mini notebooks, the practice is preserved. Kids can re-read what we practiced during reading workshop or even continue practicing when they have free time. After a quick and frequent session, this mini book goes into their book box, so that readers know just where to find it.

I don't think the brand of mini notebook matters, but I do think the size is important. Having some fun and interesting office supplies can make an arduous task a little more appealing. So I buy these books in lots of different colors and styles so kids can choose a mini book they like.

Large Thinking Boards

Over the last few years, I have implemented Thinking Boards, an idea that comes from Peter Liljedahl's book *Building Thinking Classrooms in Mathematics, Grades K-12: 14 Teaching Practices for Enhancing Learning* (2020). Currently, I have nine large whiteboard spaces in my classroom, seven of which are Wipebook Flipcharts (24"x 36"). These whiteboards are hung up permanently around the room, and children love to use them [Figure 2.5]. Often, a child and I will stand next to one of those boards to work together, or two students will collaborate and complete their quick and frequent practice on one of these vertical boards. When the work is displayed so clearly, students can showcase their learning to others in the class and explain the concept they are practicing.

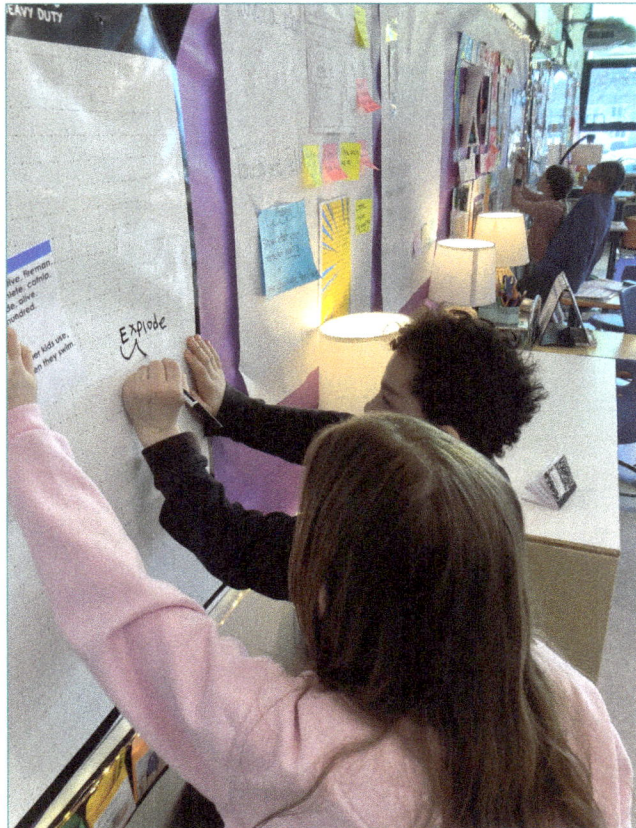

Figure 2.5
Two students play "Be the Teacher" on the Thinking Board.

High-Frequency Word Lists

I print the blank grid in Figure 2.6 on legal-size paper and students add high-frequency words as they learn them. Students use this spelling tool

_____ Spelling Tool

Aa	Bb	Cc
Dd	Ee	Ff
Gg	Hh	Ii
Jj Kk	Ll	Mm

Nn	Oo	Pp
Qq	Rr	Ss
Tt	Uu	Vv
Ww	Xx	Yy Zz

Figure 2.6

A blank high-frequency word list. When students add the words themselves, they are better able to locate them when needed. If the chart becomes too full, I exchange this chart with a typed one that lists all of the grade-level high-frequency words from the phonics curriculum. See Appendix D for a full-sized version of this spelling tool.

during writing workshop, so why not also use it to practice high-frequency words? When I want to use it during quick and frequent practice, students bring their writing folders to the table, and this chart is tucked inside it. They take the list out of their folders and read the focus words. If I want students to practice writing the words, we grab their mini composition notebooks and begin.

My other go-to resource for high-frequency word practice is Timothy Rasinski's instant phrase lists [Figure 2.7] (2016a). The words in these phrases come from Dr. Edward Fry's Instant Word List and represent about 67 percent of all the words students encounter in their reading. I enlarge these lists and students practice reading them.

Figure 2.7
Fry Instant Phrases created by Tim Rasinski.

Lists of Phonetically Regular Words, Word Sort Lists, and Photos of Word Sorts

I keep lists of phonetically regular words (organized by phonetic concept) and copies of word sort lists in small portable drawers so they are easily accessible [Figure 2.8]. I also take photos on the iPad of word sorts and building-word activities students create during whole-class phonics lessons. This gives me even more material for kids to read later. Now that my lists are all in one place (or two places—the drawers and the iPad) I can choose and easily differenti-ate what students practice. The lists I use come from the Fundations phonics program. However, if you need lists of words by phonetic concept, the free downloadables from The Six Shifts by Jan Burkins and Kari Yates are great. I

Figure 2.8
These drawers hold all of my materials for phonics. Inside each drawer are word lists, decodable texts, and materials for word sorts.

find the Short Vowels, Blends, and Digraphs Decodable Word Lists and Sentences PDF helpful [Figure 2.9].

Figure 2.9
Lists of words and sentences by phonetic concept created by Jan Burkins and Kari Yates.

Decodable Books

I have a basket of decodable books right where I work with students. I am a big fan of the Jump Rope Readers, the BEC Decodables, and the digital books from Beyond Decodables. These books are engaging, the storylines make sense, and the topics are of high interest. Reading a page or two with a student is a good amount of practice for a quick and frequent dose. Then students can add the book to their book bin to read independently or with a partner during reading workshop or a phonics lesson.

Apps

Book Widgets is another way to give kids practice with a specific phonics skill, and students love it. The website/app generates nonsense words, and the kids get to spin the wheel. I can customize the Book Widgets according to phonics skills so it is easy to click on the widget that will work best for the learners in front of me. I use this tool sporadically because the majority of the time, I want students to read real words. However, this tool is great for occasional use. At the time of this publication, a Book Widget subscription cost $49.00.

Sticky Notes

I find fun sticky notes go a long way, and I always have arrows, hearts, and lined sticky notes available for students. These grab-and-go tools give kids some places to write, and they let me label where students should stop and start reading. My advice is to never underestimate the power of office supplies. They add a little more fun to whatever the kids are doing.

All of the materials in this section are items I already have in the classroom or are easy and affordable to obtain. Additionally, I can easily adapt all of these materials to teach any of the skills I need to teach young readers and writers. To keep myself organized, I have a small shelf of drawers that holds all of these teaching tools. When I or anyone in my classroom works with a student, we just grab what we need and begin.

✔ Go-To Activities for Quick and Frequent Phonics Instruction

With all of the materials at my fingertips, implementing the Quick and Frequent Plan each week feels manageable. All I have to do now is keep the instruction engaging, purposeful, and focused. Quick and frequent phonics instruction helps kids internalize a skill and that takes many repetitions, not one long session. This is something I continually remind myself of as I teach—learning happens in many moments, not just one. Learning and practice take time, and quick and frequent practice helps kids move new learning from short-term memory into long-term.

To maximize my instructional impact when I teach phonics, I use the research about the orthographic mapping process David A. Kilpatrick outlines in *Equipped for Reading Success* to inform my instruction (2016). Kilpatrick defines orthographic mapping as the mental process we use to efficiently store words for instant, effortless retrieval (2016). He further explains:

> *We have a highly organized and efficient oral/mental filing system that allows us to instantly access the words that we hear. Our oral dictionaries are very fast. . . . The stream of sounds that we hear activates our oral/mental dictionaries. If someone speaks in an unfamiliar language, that stream of syllables is meaningless to us. Those sounds find no matches in our oral filing system.*
>
> *The big discovery regarding orthographic mapping is that this oral "filing system" is the foundation for the "filing system" we use for reading words.*
>
> *(2016, 32)*

Therefore, in many of my phonics lessons, I begin by connecting the spoken sounds in words to the corresponding graphemes. This sound work at the beginning of each phonics lesson helps children connect their oral language to the printed text. Let's take a peek at what that might look like for Sam who is learning how to read words with silent e as outlined on the Quick and Frequent Plan [Figure 2.10]. I've slowed this lesson down, so that you can see each part.

✔ What Quick and Frequent Practice Actually Looks Like—Sam

When Sam enters the classroom, he is greeted by Ms. Feeney (Kyoko Feeney, an instructional aide, who works in the classroom). She chats with him as he takes off his jacket and sits beside him at one of the small-group tables in the classroom. Sam grabs his book box and reaches for his mini composition notebook and a pencil.

Quick and Frequent Plan Week of January 9–13

NAMES	FOCUS
Sam Monday ____Tuesday ____ Wednesday ____ Thursday ____ Friday ____	**Reading** Review two sounds of each vowel—use the chart in the mini sound book Read: were, our, want, word, write, called Read a chapter in the silent e decodable book.
	Writing: Dictation: kit/kite, cap/cape, pet/Pete, hop/hope,

Figure 2.10
A Quick and Frequent Plan for Sam.

Practicing Sounds with Sam

With Sam's sound book open to the short and long vowel sound page, they begin.

"Say 'a' like in the word *cape*, says Ms. Feeney. "Please point to the letters that say the 'a' sound."

"Yes, one way to write the 'a' sound in English is 'a consonant e' [a-e]. Now say the word *cap*.

"What sound does the vowel make in *cap*?"

Sam says "ă" and points to the short "a" vowel cue card.

As Sam responds, Ms. Feeney watches and listens for which sounds and grapheme connections he knows well and which need more practice. After four or five sounds, they move onto reading or writing words.

Reading or Writing Words with Sam

"Now, let's write some of the words you said aloud. Say the word *cape*. What letters say 'ā' in the word *cape*?"

Sam responds, "a consonant e." Ms. Feeney nods and Sam writes c-a-p-e.

"Now say, *cap*," Ms. Feeney continues. "What letters spell *cap*?" Sam responds correctly and he writes c-a-p.

Ms. Feeney repeats this process with four or five words. Once Sam has written the words, he reads the words he wrote. Then he heads off to grab breakfast.

Reading or Writing Connected Text with Sam

A little later, toward the end of reading workshop, Ms. Feeney works with Sam again. "Sam, now let's see how to use what you know about short vowels and silent e as you read." She grabs the decodable book that focuses on silent e from Sam's book bin, and he reads a page or two. As he reads aloud, Ms. Feeney watches and listens to see how Sam applies these newly learned skills. Then he joins the rest of the class as they head off to recess.

Now that you've got a peek into quick and frequent phonics instruction, I'll explain each part of this practice time more and then show you what this instruction looks like for Maya and Jory.

✔ Practicing Sounds

As the earlier lesson with Sam shows, when students need to learn which graphemes represent specific sounds, I begin with the sounds, and then have the students match the sound(s) to the corresponding grapheme. Generally, I say a word and the student repeats it without seeing the word written down. Then I ask, "Which letter(s) make the sound _____?"

Depending on students' needs, I move from the simple to more complex in this way:

1. When a phonics concept is new to a student, I generally have two or three letter combinations in front of the child and ask them to point to the correct letter or letters that make that sound. When the student can successfully say and point to the corresponding letters, I add more letter combinations

from the sound book [Figure 2.3]. Having choices in front of the student is a supportive scaffold as they do not need to generate the letters on their own. Instead, they can choose from the options in front of them.

2. Once a child is proficient at saying and pointing to the correct choice, the student spells the sound aloud or writes it without the sound book in front of them. I ask, "How do you spell the _____ sound?" The child either just says the letters aloud or says the letters aloud and then writes them. I vary this practice between saying the sounds aloud and writing them to build the connection between the sounds and the graphemes.

3. Now that the student can accurately spell the sound, I combine that sound with other sounds. For example, I will ask the child to say or write a rime that incorporates the sound. "Say -ape. What letters spell -ape?" "Say -ake. What letters spell -ake?"

4. When students have more proficiency with the new skill, I combine this new phonics skill with previous learned skills and vary between reading and writing. For example, I might vary between asking, "What letters spell the sounds -ape?" "What letters spell the sound ch?" and "Which letters spell the sound br?"

When I introduce students to new phonetic concepts, I try to remember Kilpatrick's advice: "When children are involved in various literacy activities, teachers and parents should point out the relationship between what students hear in spoken words (i.e., the phonemes), and how the order of the letters matches up with the order of those oral phonemes" (2016, 53). His suggestions help me remember to build on students' oral language and move from sound to grapheme to word.

✔ Reading or Writing Words to Practice a New Phonics Skill

To internalize a phonetic concept, students must know the sound so well they can use it to both decode (read) and encode (write). Since I want to keep this individualized practice brief, I generally alternate between decoding and encoding in different teaching sessions. If we spend some time one day learning how to use the phonetic concept as a reader, the next day I will ask students to write words using the same phonetic concept. This is not a hard and fast rule, as in general I also watch and notice which modality is easier for a student. If a student has an easier time writing using the new concept, then I will spend a few days solidifying the concept through writing. Once they have an initial understanding, then I will switch to applying the concept in reading. When students read or write words, I consider the following ideas:

- Thanks to advice from Sasha Stavsky, a special education teacher with whom I collaborate daily, I am careful to choose words that focus only on the new concept and previously taught skills. For example, if a student is working on r-controlled vowels, I choose words such as *arm*, *turn*, or *firm*, not *force*. The -ce at the end of force is not a concept this student knows yet, so I stick with words that have r-controlled vowels and only letter sounds the students already know.

- When it makes sense, I also choose words that have the phonetic concept at different places in the word. *Arm*, for example, has ar at the beginning of the word, while *farm* has the same sound in the middle of the word. I want students to be flexible so the words I choose need to help them see a phonetic skill in different scenarios.

- Once students have been introduced to the new phonetic skill, I mix a few nonsense words into the practice (For example, to practice r-controlled vowels, I might give them the nonsense word *chorm*.) With some learners, it is difficult to discern whether they are reading a real word accurately because they know that particular word by sight or because they are applying the phonetic concept automatically. (Don't get me wrong, I am thrilled when kids know words by sight.) I use the nonsense words to make sure the child is actually practicing the skill I am teaching.

- Once a student can use and apply a new concept, I increase the complexity of the task in a variety of ways. I often have students read or write multisyllabic words—like *farmer* or *turning*, in the example of r-controlled vowels. I also ask students to read or write sentences that contain words that ask them to apply the concept.

- To help students remember the new phonetic skill as well as previously learned skills, I integrate words into our practice sessions from past skills. For example, if a student is learning r-controlled vowels, I will also add in some previously studied glued sounds (ung, ang, onk) as well as digraphs into the mix. When students are working with multiple skills at once, I often give them ten to fifteen word cards and let them decide how to sort them. I learn so much by watching which phonetic concepts they think about when putting the words in groups.

- When students write words, they write in their mini composition notebooks rather than with letter tiles. I like students to reread these lists and notice patterns after they are complete. If students write this sequence of words—*cat*, *cap, cape, cute, cuter*—I want them to notice what changes from word to word. Patterns easily emerge when the words are all written down.

• When kids become more proficient at reading and writing words, I turn the practice over to the kids and they play "Be the Teacher" during these practice sessions. (See Chapter 6, Quick and Frequent Moves to Help Readers Lead, to learn more.) The kids take turns leading, asking a partner to read or write specific words. As kids coach each other, I get more time to watch and notice which skills are more automatic and which need additional practice.

✔ Reading or Writing Irregular High-Frequency Words

For some students, learning irregular high-frequency words happens naturally as they read and write, while others need explicit instruction and practice to read and write these words. To teach high-frequency words, I introduce new irregularly spelled high-frequency words using the heart word magic teaching techniques Jan Burkins and Kari Yates outline in their book, *Shifting the Balance, K-2* (2021). The heart word magic teaching technique follows the orthographic mapping process to help children connect the sounds to the graphemes. Here are some tips I learned from Burkins and Yates:

1. When I teach a new word, I have the student say the word aloud and break it into phonemes. Then the student says how many phonemes are in the word. I say, "Let's learn how to read and spell the word *said*. Say the word *said*. Now, let's say all the sounds in the word. How many sounds are in the word *said*?

2. Next, I say, "Let's figure out which sounds we know how to read and spell and which parts we have to learn 'by heart.'" I say each sound and the student writes it with me. When we get to the irregular part of the word, I tell them that this is the part of the word they need to remember by heart. For *said*, the "by heart" part is the short e sound being represented with "ai."

3. Then the student says and writes the word in their mini composition notebook, placing a heart above the letters they need to remember by heart.

4. Once the word is introduced, students practice writing the word by saying each phoneme and working to remember how to spell the part they need to remember by heart.

5. Once students can read these irregular words, they review them quickly by rereading them from their mini composition book.

✔ Reading or Writing Connected Text

Students read and write daily in class during reading and writing work-shops, during our morning meeting, when we practice Reader's Theater, as part of social studies and science learning, as well as during free times. However, I also integrate a small amount of reading and writing text during their individualized instruction as I want the student to see how the phonetic skills they are learning can also be used to read and write texts. Some-times students need reminding that learning phonics will help them read the books, poems, websites, and apps they want to read. Phonics is not the end goal—proficient reading and writing of any text are the ultimate goals. Here are some quick ways I incorporate text into the quick and frequent individu-alized instruction:

1. I choose texts (songs, poems, plays, decodable books) that help stu-dents practice the phonetic skill the student is learning. Unless the text is short (one page), I don't have the student read the entire book dur-ing a quick and frequent practice session. Instead, they might read just a page at this time. Later students will read the entire book during reading workshop but not during individualized instruction. My goal during individualized instruction is to coach the student to apply the skill in text for just a few minutes so they understand why the skill is important to know.

2. So that I can find the right decodable texts when I need them, I keep them all in a drawer organized by phonetic concept [Figure 2.8]. These texts are then easy to grab when I introduce them during individualized instruction, and I give the student a copy to add to their book box to read and reread during reading workshop.

3. When a student practices writing the new phonetic concept, I often ask them to bring their writing folder to our meeting. There they add one sen-tence to the piece they are working on during writing workshop. Although the sentence the child writes isn't always a perfect match to the phonics concept they are writing, this short writing time is a great way for me to see how the student is applying previously learned phonics skills. Writing just one sentence often feels doable for the student, and it sets them up to be more independent during writing workshop because, before they close their folder, we often rehearse what they will write next.

4. When I can't easily integrate the phonetic concept into what the student is writing during writing workshop, I'll co-construct a sentence with the student using a specific keyword (e.g., "If we were going to write about

a farmer, what might we say?). Then the student writes all or part of this sentence in their mini composition notebook. Now we can reread this sentence later for practice.

I can't emphasize enough that all of these components generally *do not* happen in one sitting. Instead, more often than not, I spread these components of practice across multiple sessions. That means we might practice sounds and words in one two-minute session, and then later in the day the student reads or writes.

Now that you know a bit more about what I consider as I plan and teach the concepts listed on the Quick and Frequent Individual Plan, let's take a look at a few more examples of how this work looks and sounds in the classroom.

✔ What Quick and Frequent Phonics Practice Actually Looks Like—Jory

Let's explore an example of what might happen for Jory when she enters the classroom in the morning. I know I want to meet with Jory for a practice session as kids are coming in for the day and before the class starts our morning meeting. I have my Quick and Frequent Plan in hand [Figure 2.11] and I'm ready to go.

Quick and Frequent Plan Week of January 9–13

NAMES	FOCUS
Jory Monday ____ Tuesday ____ Wednesday ____ Thursday ____ Friday ____	**Reading** Read: what, after, now, want Read a chapter in the blends decodable book. Read: strong, cluck, mask, mend, slant **Writing:** Dictation: desk, mask, pond, skunk, last

Figure 2.11
A Quick and Frequent Plan for Jory

After Jory puts away her things and finishes breakfast, she joins me at my small-group table with her book box she reads from during reading workshop. I begin. "Good morning, Jory. Did you get to play softball last night? How did it go?" (Jory often spends her evenings on a field.)

"Hey, Jory, let's practice those tricky words. You have learned so many already and these are just a few more tricky ones." She grabs her mini composition book from her book box and I point to the words *why*, *because*, *right*, *between*, and *other* as Jory reads them. I notice that Jory reads all of them accurately except *other*. I write that one down in my notes.

"Wow!" I exclaim. You know so many of these words. Tomorrow let's heart map the word *other* so you know that one by heart too.

Next, I ask Jory to write the words *strong*, *cluck*, *mask*, *mend*, and *slant* in her mini composition notebook. Before she writes a word, she says the sounds aloud. Then I choose a sound or cluster of sounds and ask, "How do you spell the sounds _____?"

After writing the words, Jory reads them and points out the end blends. As she gets up to leave, I remind Jory to keep looking through the whole word so her eyes see the blend at the end of a word. I put a sticky note on this page in her mini composition notebook, and she places it back in her book box. Then she puts her book box away and returns to her table to clean up her breakfast. I jot a note in my conferring notebook to record my observations, and I am off to another quick and frequent practice session with another student.

Later in the day when Mrs. Feeney, an instructional aide, has a free moment, she will pull Jory aside and they will repeat this work or choose something else from the Quick and Frequent Plan to work on. Honestly, any and all of the activities listed will help Jory read and write blends so I don't care what she chooses. Jory needs continual practice to internalize this skill and she is getting it.

Tomorrow morning Jory will come to my table again, and on this day we will read the words in the mini composition notebook that she wrote yesterday. Then she will read a chapter from her decodable book, and we will practice reading end blends in context. By the end of the week, Jory will have completed all of these activities multiple times, and I will be able to see which skills need to be repeated the next week and which skills she now knows automatically.

✔ What Quick and Frequent Practice Actually Looks Like—Maya

As Jory heads off to do the morning routines, I grab Maya's book box and sit beside her as she finishes up her breakfast.

Quick and Frequent Plan Week of January 9–13

NAMES	FOCUS
Maya Monday ____Tuesday ____ Wednesday ____ Thursday ____ Friday ____	**Reading:** Practice i and u short vowel sounds—use the chart in the mini sound book Read digraph word cards Read *Jack at Bat*
	Writing: Dictation: chop, chip, chap, check, much

Figure 2.12
A Quick and Frequent Plan for Maya.

"Good morning, Maya. It is so good to see you this morning. How did things go with your brother this morning?" (Maya often tells stories about helping her younger brother get ready for school.)

"Let's practice those vowel sounds and read a page together before the day begins. I grab the mini sound book with visuals and say, "What vowel makes the sound _____?" Maya repeats the sound and points to the corresponding vowel.

"Wow! Look at you, Maya. You remembered the sounds of a, i, e, and o. Just u is still tricky. Good for you. Let's read a page in this book so you can practice using those sounds as you read."

She finishes reading the book page, and I say, "Did you see how quickly you are solving words? You are looking at all the letters in the words and blending the sounds together." Now Maya heads off to clean up her breakfast and put her book box away, and I bring the class together for the morning meeting.

✔ Go-To Times of Day for Quick and Frequent Phonics Practice

Sneaking in quick and frequent practice sessions can be tricky as we want all kids to enjoy the few moments of social time available in transition times throughout the day and spend the majority of their time reading and writing texts they love. Here are my go-to times of the day for two- to five-minute small instructional bursts.

Before Morning Meeting

After September, kids complete the morning routine in my class independently. They put their things away, eat breakfast, order lunch, and then have a few minutes to explore something in the classroom—reading, writing, drawing, exploring the science table, or chatting with friends.

While that morning routine is happening, I have a few minutes to greet kids, check in with those who may need some individual attention, and work with one or two students. "It is so good to see you. Let's take just two minutes to practice _____." I often end with some explicit feedback. "I noticed that _____ was much easier for you to remember. What did you notice?" I jot down a quick note and move on to the next student.

Right Before a Transition

The class is about to wrap up one part of learning and move on to another part of the day. As the class cleans up and transitions, I take a couple of minutes to work with one or two students. I call these students over and get them started with some practice. When they are almost done, I transition the whole class to the next part of the day. The students finish up and join us for the start of the next lesson. When this works well, I am so pleased. The kids have missed very little instructional time, and I have snuck in another practice session.

Any Extra Help

When the principal sends an email explaining that there is someone in the building who can help in classrooms, my response is immediate. Absolutely. I would love the help. I will take anyone who is free at any time the kids are in the classroom. Since I have the Quick and Frequent Plan ready and the materials all in one place, it is easy for someone to sit beside a student to complete a practice session. All it takes is a brief explanation from me, and then they are off and running. Now I can keep teaching as they work with students individually. To help me keep track of what has been done and how students did, I have the guest teacher highlight any miscues the student made and check off what they completed on the plan. This way, I know where to pick back up. If the teacher works in my room consistently, they have access to an Excel spreadsheet where they keep notes [Figure 1.4].

During Small-Group Instruction

As students transition to the table for small-group instruction, I often have one of these quick and frequent activities out and ready to go. Sometimes, I have two children working on Book Widget for one minute, while I read with another child. At other times, I watch students practice in their mini composition books while others read a page from a decodable text. Then they switch. After these two minutes of practice are over, I begin my small-group lesson.

During small groups, I have to make sure the quick and frequent practice work doesn't take up my entire small-group lesson time. I want to make sure I have adequate time to teach students a strategy and have them read and write authentically while I am by their side. Since my entire small-group lesson is generally no longer than ten minutes, I need to keep the quick and frequent practice component short. The kids have lots to learn, and reviewing phonetic skills is just one piece of their learning.

Unexpected Times

Sometimes you find a time that you couldn't anticipate. One year I had a student who ate lunch quickly and was just sitting there during the last five minutes of lunch. It was in the earlier days of Covid, and kids were spaced far apart so it wasn't a social time. Instead of waiting in the cafeteria, he came up to the classroom three minutes before the class arrived. We used this time as a daily practice session and wrapped up as the rest of the class entered. You might find an unexpected tiny pocket of time in your day as well—whether it's a regular time or just an occasional one. When you have a solid Quick and Frequent Plan in place, you'll know how to use these tiny pockets when they appear.

Now, when I look into my kids' eyes during whole-group phonics time, I am less worried. Maya, Jory, and Sam (and any other student who needs it) receive targeted phonics instruction designed for them throughout the school day. This individualized work is helping to teach them the foundational phonics skills they need to read, and the daily whole-class phonics instruction is helping them learn grade-level material. Not everything goes perfectly every day, but it is better. As their phonetic knowledge becomes stronger, the easier it will be for these students to learn more complex skills. Then, as these skills become automatic, these kids will use their foundational knowledge to solve unfamiliar words strategically and comprehend the meaning of the text. During writing, they will move toward writing words with short vowels, blends, and even silent e accurately. I will also see them reach for their mini sound books independently and use this tool to help themselves when they need support. The quick and frequent practice is helping them develop their skills, build their confidence, and make reading and writing a more joyful experience.

For me, the joy of this process comes from watching the kids in action. Quick and frequent instruction gives me more opportunities to understand what my students know, and where they need to go next. I learn so much in these two- to five-minute bursts of individual and small-group instruction. However, to keep the momentum in the classroom going, I have to remember to keep it simple. It is when I add too many learning goals that I become overwhelmed and have trouble sticking with the plan. When I follow my own advice, the quick and frequent plan eases my mind, as I know that I am actively working to support each learner.

3

Quick and Frequent Fluency Moves

Maya runs into the classroom one morning. "Mrs. Mulligan, I can't get this song out of my head. I just love it so much!"

"Maya, what is the name of the song?" I ask. "I can't wait to listen to it. If the song works for a school audience, would you like to share it with the class?"

Maya begins to sing. "You can count on me like one, two, three," and I already know that this Bruno Mars song will resonate with the kids.

The next day, Maya shares the song with the class and hands out copies of the lyrics. Then she projects the chorus onto the whiteboard from the document camera and proceeds to read the lyrics to the class, while the rest of the students follow along.

If you watched Maya share this song, you might see a disconnect between what her reading assessment data reveals [Figure 2.1] and how she reads in this moment. Maya is currently a word-by-word reader, who generally doesn't volunteer to read aloud. As a second grader, she knows approximately thirty out of ninety of the first-grade high-frequency words and very few of the second-grade words. Her lack of automaticity with these words is one reason her reading is slow and labored.

As we know, readers and people are complex. Maya can both struggle with fluency as a reader and be hesitant to read aloud *and* thrive as a fluent reader in certain contexts. My goal is to help Maya (and all readers) develop strong fluency that will support them in reading whatever texts they choose to read.

Reading and singing song lyrics is just another way for Maya and the rest of the class to practice reading high-frequency words and reading with expression while also learning new vocabulary and thinking about deeper meanings in a text. In their article, "Let's Bring Back the Magic of Song for Teaching Reading," Becky Iwasaki, Timothy Rasinski, Kasim Yildirim, and Belinda S. Zimmerman write,

> *A growing body of research and scholarly thought suggests that singing has potential for improving reading (Biggs, Homan, Dedrick, & Rasinski, 2008; Fisher, 2001; Harp, 1988; Hines, 2010; Miller & Coen, 1994; Smith, 2000). For example, Biggs and colleagues (2008) found that the regular repeated singing and reading of songs by struggling middle school readers over a nine-week period resulted in significantly greater progress in reading achievement (seven months gain on average) than a comparison group of students in an alternative intervention.*

> *(2013, 137–138)*

Song lyrics are a text that students enjoy rereading, and they are a natural quick and frequent practice that builds reading skills and also brings joy. Instead of rereading solely being a way to correct miscues, rereading now becomes what readers do when they love a text. Singing songs again and again is part of the fun, and once the children have sung a song a few times they generally know the words. Then we can use the song lyrics for comprehension work, as students have lots to share about the deeper meanings of songs. Their hands-down conversations (see Chapter 4 for more on this conversation structure) help them to learn new vocabulary and to think about what the song is really about. These repeated readings, and the way song lyrics sometimes stick in our minds, help students to ponder possible meanings of the text, listen to their peers' interpretations, and, through conversation, build comprehension skills. Yet one of the most critical elements of song singing in the classroom is that kids see practice as a kind of fun we have together in the classroom.

However, at this moment, Maya isn't thinking about the instructional possibilities of sharing song lyrics with the group. She is thrilled that she can lead the class, and I am grateful. Maya is taking the lead—a much needed literacy leadership moment. I hope moments like these will stay with her and help her to persevere when reading is difficult.

✔ Using Songs to Promote Fluency

Our daily song routine is quite simple. On Monday mornings, students glue a copy of a new song into their community notebook (a composition book that holds poems, plays, and songs we read together). Then, to call the class to the carpet for morning meeting, instead of ringing a chime or asking for their attention, I play the music. (I credit this routine to Debbie Miller as I remember watching her students transitioning with music in her teaching videos.)

Every morning, as soon as students hear the music, students grab their community notebook and head to the rug for morning meeting. I love the way they help each other find the appropriate page in their notebooks, all eager to come together as a group for singing. Once we are all gathered, I start the song again, and students point to the words in their notebooks and sing along. Then, as the song is playing, and the class is singing, I move around the group, supporting kids to match speech to text.

For striving readers, this matching of speech to text is tricky initially. On those first days, they often have a hard time listening and following along. But that changes as the week progresses and the tune becomes "stuck in their heads." By Wednesday, generally, they have got it, and the smiles as they sing along are priceless.

To help readers learn the lyrics, I generally play the same song all week. Yes, I play it at morning meetings when students have their community notebooks, but I also play it during many transitions when they don't have the words in front of them. During these moments, I project a lyric video of the song onto the board so that they can read along as they sing. Students don't even seem to notice how many times they are reading this song throughout the week. They are concentrating on singing with their peers.

For Maya, and many other children, the melody makes reading these complex texts a whole lot easier. Sometimes students already know the chorus of the song, and if they don't, by the end of the week they have learned it by heart. In the morning meeting they use this knowledge to match their spoken words to the printed words on the page. Then, during reading workshop, I encourage students to reread the new song or any of the past common texts. Their community notebooks stay right in their reading book boxes so these texts are right at their fingertips.

Choosing Songs

The songs we sing each week come from a variety of different sources. Like the song Maya recommended, the children themselves are a great source for songs. I have to explain that sometimes a song they love can be amazing, but it isn't right for school. That doesn't mean there is anything wrong with their choice—it might be that a song is about a grown-up topic or uses words we don't say at school. If this happens to a student, I will let them look at my collection of songs from past years and select one of those that they would like to sing with the class.

Collaborating with the music teacher is another way I find songs kids love. Especially at the beginning of the year, if I can tap into the music teacher's selections, then the children get even more exposure to the songs.

I am careful to choose songs by artists of all different backgrounds and who write different types of music. I choose songs that will promote conversations about peace, kindness, self-advocacy, and social justice. Since the song lyrics have become a common text in the classroom, I want the lyrics and the accompanying videos to be thought-provoking so that students can ponder deeper meanings and listen to others' perspectives. Once we have sung a song a few times and students are familiar with the words, we will talk about the lyrics during a hands-down conversation (Chapter 4). I find the more I can use texts in multiple ways in the classroom, the deeper students' understanding becomes. These multiple exposures give them time to think about a text in new ways. Here are some of my go-to resources for songs.

Playing for Change

Playing for Change is a curated selection of music videos that celebrate peace and social justice. Through watching these videos, children see people from all around the world creating music together. These videos not only spark joyful singing (and conga lines parading around the classroom!), they also invite students to talk about inclusion, diversity, and the power of learning about others. My second graders repeatedly asked to hear "Love Train" featuring Jason Mraz, Chad Smith, and Yo-Yo Ma again and again [Figure 3.1].

Figure 3.1
"Love Train," one of my class's favorite songs from Playing for Change.

Dance for Kindness

My kids and I are pretty obsessed with the Dance for Kindness videos [Figure 3.2]. These montages show people from around the world all dancing the same choreographed dance to celebrate kindness. The music is filled with big messages about giving to others and believing in yourself, and the dancers are from different age groups, abilities, and backgrounds. This yearly initiative is a beautiful example of the best ways our diverse world can come together to impact others. Since these videos are longer (seven minutes) and contain multiple songs, I choose one song from the video to focus on for our weekly singing.

Figure 3.2
The Dance for Kindness website.

We Are Teachers

This post [Figure 3.3] by Meghan Mathis titled "The Big List of School-Appropriate Songs to Keep Everyone Pumped Up and Motivated" has some great titles (2023).

Figure 3.3
Megan Mathis's Big List of School-Appropriate Songs.

It is also easy to access these songs right from the We Are Teachers Spotify page. Kids ask to hear these songs again and again in the classroom, and families tell me that their children ask to listen at home too.

Hopscotch

Some weeks I choose songs with curricular connections or topics that interest kids. When I want a song to help students remember the names of the continents or the oceans, I turn to Joanna and Matt Pace's songs on Hopscotchsongs. com [Figure 3.4]. This teacher and musician team create songs with catchy tunes and information-packed lyrics.

Figure 3.4
Hopscotch is a great resource for educational songs.

Number Rock Math Music Videos

My students also love many of the songs from Number Rock [Figure 3.5]. They love the tunes, and I often hear them saying the lyrics aloud when solving math problems. One of their all-time favorite tunes is "Types of Lines." The music is pretty catchy, and the hand movements bring the concepts to life. Please note that this website does have a monthly subscription cost.

Figure 3.5
The Number Rock Math Music Video website.

Mrs. Siravo YouTube Channel

The kids think these music video parodies [Figure 3.6] are hysterical, and as they watch they learn some essential phonics rules. The "Consonant le Syllables" video, sung to the tune of the Backstreet Boys song, "I Want It That Way," is a class favorite.

Figure 3.6
Mrs. Siravo's phonics parodies.

Before printing the lyrics of next week's song, I play portions of it during a few transitions the week prior so I can watch kids' reactions. Sometimes they run over to me with excitement, and other times they groan with disappointment. And, of course, I get all reactions in between. When I find a song that seems to resonate with the group, then I'll print the lyrics so students can glue them into their community notebooks.

Depending on the song lyrics, sometimes I make the decision to print just the chorus. I try to balance keeping the text level challenging and making sure the text isn't too long. I typically scan the lyrics to analyze the text difficulty, and then I also pay attention to the pace of the song. If the song is very fast, just having the chorus might help readers read and sing along. Then, with other songs, I give them all the words to stretch their learning. Generally, as the year progresses, the songs get more complex, but more importantly, I make these decisions based on the kids in front of me. I always want to keep in mind that when kids are enthusiastic about what we are doing, they won't even notice how much they are practicing. Singing songs daily takes less than five minutes, and that makes it another small move. However, what is even more important is the feeling that comes over the classroom when our voices are together. It is a sign that our community is bonding and reading skills are growing.

✔ Using Reader's Theater to Promote Fluency

About midway through the year, once all readers have a better grasp on their foundational skills, our quick and frequent fluency work continues and expands to include Reader's Theater.

> *Reader's Theater is an oral activity in which students read scripts or stories (after practicing reading their particular part and gaining assistance as necessary with vocabulary, phrasing, expressiveness, etc.). Each student takes the part of one of the characters or narrator. There is no need for an actual production of a play or theatrical event although props may be used.*
>
> *(Rasinski 2016b)*

To complete this work, I generally follow the steps outlined in Rasinski and Young's fluency research that they shared in an online workshop titled, "A Step-by-Step Guide to Fluency Instruction in the Age of SOR" (2023). Their step-by-step approach to repeated readings fits right into quick and frequent practice:

Reader's Theater Step-by-Step (Rasinski and Young 2023):

Monday: *The teacher models fluent reading of the Reader's Theater text, and students choose a text.*

Tuesday: *The teacher selects a part of the text and teaches decoding strategies.*

Wednesday: *The teacher teaches a minilesson on reading with expression, and the students practice.*

Thursday: *Students have a final practice session.*

Friday: *Students perform their Reader's Theater plays.*

Each of these steps takes about ten minutes to complete, and as a class, we dive into it right after morning meeting. Here is how Reader's Theater quick and frequent practice works:

On Monday, I read aloud two different texts to the group, and they follow along on copies of the text. Once students have heard each short play, students put their name on the text they would like to perform. They return the texts to me, and before the end of the day, I organize everyone into performance groups. I frequently do not assign parts as I like the kids to negotiate this among themselves, but depending on group dynamics and reading levels, I sometimes assign parts so that each child's quick and frequent practice matches what they need to learn.

The next day (generally Tuesday, but not always), students meet in their assigned small groups based on the play they chose. (Generally, no more than four kids in a group.) This means that multiple groups are performing the same plays.

If I have not assigned roles, students begin by deciding who will read each part. Then they read their lines independently and glue their scripts into their community notebooks. As groups read and practice their lines independently, I support the readers who need additional help decoding unfamiliar words.

Since these Reader's Theater scripts are grade-level texts, some children need to practice more than others, and that is just what I want because the frequent practice helps striving readers internalize new vocabulary and learn more high-frequency words, as well as build their fluency skills. After students glue their script into their community notebook it stays in their book boxes, and students can reread their lines during reading workshop. When kids need more support, I will add reading the script to the Quick and Frequent Plan, and then during my two- to five-minute instructional bursts, they will practice their lines.

When it makes sense for certain students, I also send scripts home for additional practice. I've even given a few students the scripts to take home the week prior to working on it in class because it works best for some students to look over the texts with a grown-up at home and choose a part that they will love. Sometimes, I adjust the typical timeline and we will practice a script for a week and a half or two weeks. If students reread a grade-level text for a couple more days, they are still getting the practice they need. I keep in mind that the goal of this work is joyful fluent reading, and I adjust my teaching moves as needed.

On Wednesday, I kick off our Reader's Theater work with a whole-class fluency lesson. Sometimes we discuss how to infer the way a character in the script is feeling and read the dialogue to reflect that feeling. Other times, I might emphasize the importance of noticing and reading punctuation to bring out the meaning. During other weeks, I emphasize how to say words in meaningful phrases to help the audience comprehend the play. Then, once again, readers set off to practice their lines in their small groups and give each other pointers to improve their fluency.

Thursday is all about getting ready for the performance. Students practice independently, and then with their Reader's Theater group. They are encouraged to think about what is happening in the text and make their voices match the characters' feelings. Students are also invited to add hand gestures and small actions to bring the play to life.

Generally, Friday is "performance day." My quotes here are intentional. The word performance often evokes images of costumes, props, and a stage—our performances do not have all that fanfare. Instead, readers simply bring their plays to life with fluent reading, hand gestures, and expressive voices. Generally, the groups "perform" to one or two people. Our first several weeks of performances are to adults. I'll ask specialist teachers, administrators, custodians—anyone who might have a free moment to pop by to see a five-minute performance. Then, when someone shows up at the classroom door, one group goes out into the hallway and performs. This happens in an organic way throughout the day until all groups have had a turn.

After several weeks of performing various Reader's Theater texts for adults, I'll ask another grade level if the kids can perform for a few of their students in small groups. For these performances, the entire class heads down to the grade level's classrooms, and then a couple of kids from each classroom come into the hallway to watch. Then I spread the groups out down the hallway or into an empty classroom and the performances happen simultaneously. When one group finishes early, they just join another group and listen to their peers perform.

So that grown-ups at home can see a performance, I ask one of the adults who is watching to record it on the classroom iPad. Then, all I have to do is upload the video to Seesaw and the people at home can enjoy it too. Just to be clear, I do not record student performances every week. Instead, I record two performances. I video the first time we do Reader's Theater because the kids are so excited, and then I video one of their last performances. This way kids and families can see the growth over time.

To me, the whole Reader's Theater process is simple because it only takes ten to fifteen minutes a day. It fits into our weekly routine without too much difficulty. Keeping it quick and frequent means that I can sustain this fluency practice over time so that kids build these essential skills in joyful ways.

Finding Texts for Reader's Theater

When looking for plays, I follow the same guidelines I use when I select any other read-aloud. I think about the qualities of the text and am careful to choose scripts that have authentic representations of people from diverse backgrounds and plotlines that promote conversations about point of view, diversity, and inclusion. In the book, *Conscious Classroom*, Allison Briceño and Claudia Rodriguez-Mojica list important questions for educators to consider when selecting texts (2022). I use these questions when I choose any text to read aloud, including the texts I use for Reader's Theater. Here are some of the questions they suggest educators consider when selecting texts:

1. *Do the author and illustrator have lived experiences the book seeks to represent?*
2. *Is the copyright date after 1973?*
3. *Do the illustrations represent stereotypes?*
4. *Is the storyline respectful to all?*
5. *Are diverse characters represented as stereotypes?*
6. *Are the characters human?*
7. *From what perspective is the author writing?*
8. *Whose historical or cultural perspective is told or valued?*
9. *Are there characters with whom children can positively self-identify?*

   (Briceño and Rodriguez-Mojica 2022, 68–71)

After I consider these questions, I also think carefully about text complexity. Reader's Theater is an opportunity for all students to read grade-level text, and since they are rereading their parts four to six times, the text should be challenging. There should be opportunities to learn new vocabulary and become more automatic with high-frequency words. At the same time, I don't want the text to be so challenging that all readers can't read a part fluently with practice. After three readings, I want the readers to feel successful and fluent in their reading. Of course, this all becomes more complicated because our classrooms are filled with a wide range of readers.

This is why I choose short scripts or poems, and I give readers a choice of text. (Recall that on Mondays I read aloud two options and then readers self-select what is right for them.) The majority of the time, readers choose well. However, if someone feels frustrated with their lines, it is easy to switch them to a different part of another play. This practice is meant to be short and joyful, and having a few options makes it easy to adapt in the moment.

Finding texts that meet all these criteria can be tricky. Many of the resources available for Reader's Theater online are dated. This is why I expand my options to include poetry, poetry for two voices, stories, and actual scripts. Here are a few resources I use for finding high-quality texts for Reader's Theater.

- One of my favorite resources is the poetry anthology, *Messing Around on the Monkey Bars and Other School Poems for Two Voices*. This poetry book by Betsy Franco and Jessie Hartland is one of the most popular books in my class. Kids are eager to grab and read this text after I model how to read poems in two voices with a partner. As I watch kids explore the book, I note their favorite poems, and these become options for future Reader's Theater.

- Pioneer Valley Books has created Reader's Theater plays based on stories about their beloved dog characters, Bella, Rose, Jack, and Daisy. These books are written at text complexities F–J and can be purchased as single copies.

- Learning for Justice's website has a collection of perspective texts appropriate for a variety of grade levels. These short texts can be sorted by text complexity and genre. While these texts are not written as scripts, they are easily adapted. After I read the text aloud, it is easy for the class to write the character's name next to a line. This is important work for kids to do as they have to think about who is speaking.

- Dr. Chase Young's website has a large selection of Reader's Theater scripts listed under the RTscripts tab. Many of these scripts are familiar stories that kids know and love. There are many traditional tales that match perfectly with a second-grade unit of study. Some of the kids' favorites are the nonfiction plays about animals. They just love performing these plays. and they are great mentor texts as kids consider writing their own Reader's Theater play during writing workshop. As with any resource, please be a careful consumer when choosing texts.

- Poetry anthologies are great resources for Reader's Theater. Although these texts are not written for two voices, students love to read them aloud. Sometimes students decide to read a poem in unison, other times they alternate reading lines or stanzas. When I let the kids figure out how to perform these poems, their ideas are creative and engaging for the audience. Here are a few anthologies that I rely on:

  - *Hip Hop Speaks to Children: A Celebration of Poetry with a Beat*, edited by Nikki Giovanni. After I introduce this text, I can't get this book out of kids' hands. They sit on the rug during their free time perusing the anthology and listening to the accompanying CD. There are so many choices for performances, and it is an opportunity to introduce kids to poets such as Eloise Greenfield, Langston Hughes, and Nikki Giovanni.

- *Just Like Me* by Vanessa Brantley-Newton. This anthology is filled with poems featuring girls. The different poems tell mini stories about these girls, their lives, and their feelings.

- *No Voice Too Small: Fourteen Young Americans Making History*, edited by Lindsay H. Metcalf, Keila V. Dawson, and Jeanette Bradley. This collection of poems introduces readers to young activists who stand up for their beliefs and details how readers can also make a difference. I organize partnerships based on which people in the book different kids are most interested in learning about. This way, kids with common interests have an opportunity to work and read together.

- *Read! Read! Read!*, written by Amy Ludwig Vanderwater and illustrated by Ryan O'Rourke. From reading maps and road signs to exploring the deep feelings that emerge when reading stories, Amy Ludwig Vanderwater has a poem about it. Kids choose whether to read these poems by alternating stanzas, lines, or chorally reading together.

- Poetry picture books are also great texts for Reader's Theater. Partners can chorally read the text or take turns reading pages. I have a basket of these books in the classroom and partners love to choose a favorite and practice together. Here are a few favorites:

  - *A Place Inside of Me: A Poem to Heal the Heart*, by Zetta Elliott and illustrated by Noa Denmom. This powerful poem is written about a child's feelings throughout a year, as he and his community grieve after a police shooting.

  - *She Persisted: 13 Women Who Changed the World*, by Chelsea Clinton. This book introduces kids to a diverse group of women who stood up for their beliefs. The repeated refrain makes it easy for kids to read the text and understand the deeper meanings. Kids can choose to read aloud about just a few people or chorally read the entire picture book.

  - *Change Sings: A Children's Anthem*, by Amanda Gorman and illustrated by Loren Long. This beautiful poem is about working together to make the world a better place, and the illustrations depict children helping others. When children read this text during Reader's Theater, two students work together and they alternate reading the pages.

In my classroom, I use all of these resources but not all at the same time. I watch the learners and decide whether a song, a poem, or Reader's Theater script is the best choice for where we are on a learning journey as a class. Just like many of you, I have required units to teach, and I try to integrate this fluency work into what we are learning in the content areas. I also connect this work with Learning for Justice's Social Justice Standards (and the four domains of identity, diversity, justice, and action) (2023). I choose poems, songs, short stories, or Reader's Theater scripts that support these goals.

At the beginning of the year, I usually start with songs and short poems as these kinds of texts are particularly good for building classroom community. Then, during the middle of the year, I'll move to more complex poetry and perspective texts interspersed with some new songs. As the spring approaches, the Reader's Theater scripts become a more prominent part of our work as so many of them connect with our traditional tales unit of study. Finally, at the end of the year, we delve even deeper into perspective texts and take some of our favorite picture book read-alouds from the year and turn those into scripts.

I find having these resources all at my fingertips lets me be responsive to the needs and interests of the students in front of me. For example, one day, I watched Maya during a writing block as she struggled to write the word *teammate*. As I watched her grab a mini sound book to choose a spelling for the vowel team, I heard her humming the chorus and swaying her body to Andy Grammer's song, "Keep Your Head Up." Even though the spelling problem in front of her was challenging, Maya was using this song to help her persevere.

Singing together and performing Reader's Theater is a quick and frequent fluency practice that adds so much joy to the classroom. What I love most is watching how students eagerly reread these texts even when they have free moments during the day.

4

Quick and Frequent Comprehension Moves (Ways to Deepen Conversations About Text)

I sit beside Jory as she sounds out the word *switch*. She's got the "sw" on her paper. Then she stops and looks at me. I point to her mini sound book [Figure 2.3] and she grabs it in frustration. "Why can't I ever remember anything," Jory groans.

"Jory, can I tell you something I've noticed about you as a reader?" I ask. She gives me an unconvincing nod. "There are lots of parts of learning to read, and you are so strong at some parts, and other parts are tricky right now. Did you hear yourself during our hands-down conversation today? Look at what you wrote on this sticky note." I say [Figure 4.1].

"That's not reading," Jory mumbles.

I take a breath before responding, so I can better hide my disappointment about what she just said. "Jory, thinking deeply is one of the most important parts of reading. Would you do me a favor?"

She gives me an unconvincing nod once again.

"Please notice your thinking during read-aloud. I want you to see your brilliant ideas. When you notice what you do well, it can help you work through the very hard parts of reading. You won't always have trouble remembering your sounds. With lots of practice, you will know them by heart. The amazing

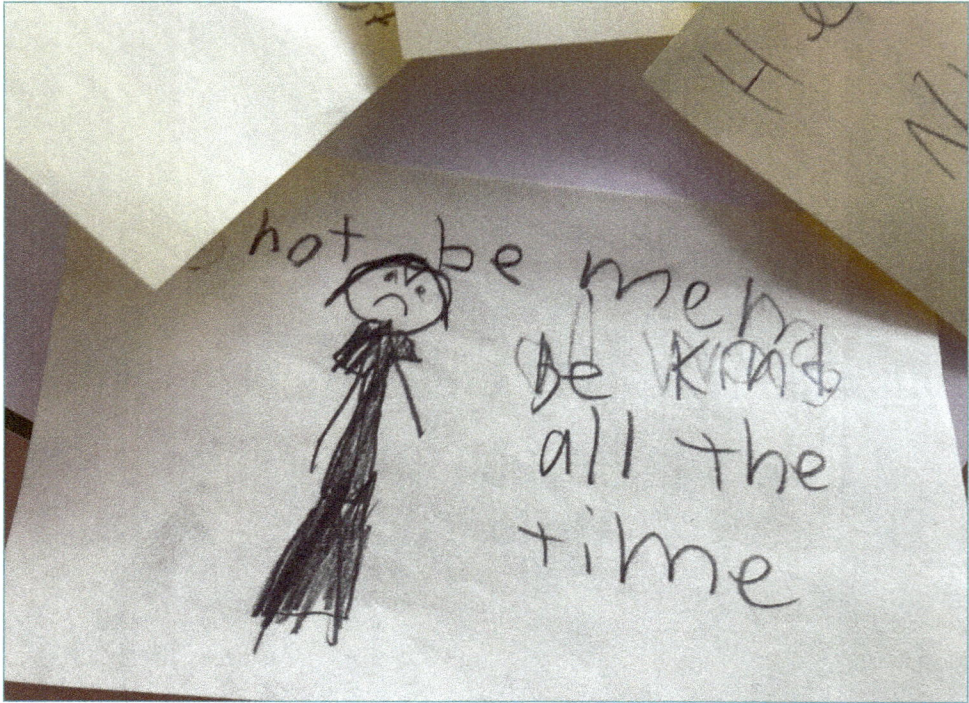

Figure 4.1
Jory's sticky note from a hands-down conversation that reads "Do not be mean/Be kind all the time."

thing about thinking is that your ideas will continue to grow and change throughout your whole life. Jory, I know you can do hard things because I see you work hard every day."

✔ What Are Hands-Down Conversations?

While learning and practicing foundational reading skills like phonics are critical components of learning to read, they aren't the only important parts. Students must have ample opportunities to think about the meaning of texts and engage in conversations about this meaning with peers. One way we engage in this practice in my classroom is through a discussion structure called hands-down conversations. A hands-down conversation is a discussion students have as a whole class (and eventually in small groups) without raising their hands. Students watch, notice, listen, and speak naturally, similar to a grown-up book club—or a kid version of a grown-up conversation.

Hands-down conversations are primarily student-led, and through these experiences, students learn many conversational moves. They practice looking at the speaker, listening to what someone says in order to build on their ideas, changing or "growing" their ideas, deepening their understanding, and thinking about a text or an idea from multiple points of view. Here is a snippet of my students' hands-down conversation after I read aloud *Big Boys Cry* by Jonty Howley.

After I finished reading aloud the book, Sam spoke out first, "I think the dad made a mistake because he cried at the end of the book. He shouldn't have said, 'big boys don't cry.' It isn't true."

Then Jory adds, "Sam, I heard you say that the dad made a mistake and I agree. It is okay to cry."

Maya asks a question. "Sam, what makes you think that?"

Sam adds, "In the story, all of the men cry. They are all crying for different reasons."

I chime in and ask, "Sam brings up an important point. Why were the characters crying? Was it for the same reasons or different ones?"

A student reaches for the book and opens to the ending. "See. Right here the dad is crying because he was worried when his son went away."

Another student takes the book and opens to the beginning. "I think the dad and the boy are crying for the same reason—they both missed each other."

Some students are connecting the beginning and the end of the book, and that is great progress toward deeply understanding texts. Yet, at the same time, I notice wiggly bodies and decide to end the conversation for the day. I promise to reread the book tomorrow so we can think together about the lessons the author Jonty Howley might be teaching his readers.

Hands-down conversations are a quick and frequent practice for connecting readers with one another to do the work of comprehension. Through conversations that are centered on students' ideas, these small moments across the year add up as students learn to explain their ideas about the text, consider new perspectives, and so much more.

Many literacy leaders in the field include hands-down conversations (commonly called accountable talk) with students as part of the interactive read-aloud practice, and this discussion structure is described so well in many professional texts. To learn more about interactive read-aloud from others in the field, refer to these texts:

- *Unlocking the Power of Classroom Talk: Teaching Kids to Talk with Clarity & Purpose*, by Shana Frazin and Katy Wischow. This book is filled with practical ideas for how to lift the level of talk so that students can build relationships, play with ideas, clarity, analyze, argue, and report.

- *Building Bigger Ideas: A Process for Teaching Purposeful Talk*, by Maria Nichols. The coaching tips in this book for how to honor what students are doing and also teach and elevate students' talking skills are helpful.

- *Hands Down Speak Out: Listening and Talking Across Literacy and Math K-5*, by Kassia Omohundro Wedekind and Christy Hermann Thompson. This book is written in a lesson-plan format making it easy to find the topics you need to teach and try them out in the classroom.

Hands-down conversations are my number one move for teaching students to infer the deeper meanings of a text. They take about five to seven minutes once or twice a week. I use this conversation structure when we read a text that resonates with students, a social problem arises and the class wants to solve it (e.g., the playground balls are not getting put away at the end of recess), or there is a question the group wants to ponder (e.g., Maya broke her arm and we want to support her. What are some ways we can help?).

The frequency of hands-down conversations varies throughout the year. At the beginning of the year, the conversations are daily and last only two to three minutes because students need quick and frequent practice to understand this new discussion format, and we can use hands-down conversations to make lots of decisions as a class community (e.g., what classroom jobs should we have? Or what will we do when we disagree?). Then, throughout the rest of the year, hands-down conversations happen about once or twice a week. One conversation a week is about a read-aloud we loved, and the other conversations might be about a person we met during "Meet Someone New" (see Chapter 5) or a social-emotional topic like how fair and equal are the same in some situations and very different in others (making sure everyone gets to use the chalk is very different from who has access to a wobbly stool in class).

These quick and frequent conversations may be short, but they have big impacts. Children take the lead, and they learn from each other. They learn to actively listen, consider other perspectives, and share their own ideas. Most importantly, they learn that revising your ideas is a smart thing to do. They integrate new ideas with their current understanding and grow new thinking. Isn't this what learning is all about?

Just think about the times in your life when you spoke with someone else about a text. Remember those moments when you listened to someone else's ideas and thought, "I never thought of that," or "I didn't notice…" Then, the next time you read, you noticed more because of that previous conversation. Perhaps you gained a new perspective, learned about a new resource, thought about the symbolism in a text, or pondered the significance of the title. It was that conversation that strengthened your understanding and your comprehension and allowed you to notice something new. It's the same for kids too. The brilliance is that these conversations transcend literacy and become part of all curriculum areas. Kids have hands-down conversations about their learning in literacy science, math, social studies, as well as so many aspects of social-emotional learning.

Another benefit of having quick and frequent hands-down conversations once or twice a week is that they save hours of time later in the school year. Since the kids know how to have productive conversations, they apply this new skill when talking with a partner, running their own book clubs, and working in cooperative groups. The children know how to listen, share talking time, and disagree respectfully. I don't need to teach these lessons as I launch book clubs, or when children plan a science experiment. Instead, I can focus on the complex thinking work students do, because the kids already know how to talk in groups. These conversations are one way to let kids take the lead because they let us listen to what they know and understand. What could be better than that? And it all happens in these quick two- to five-minute bursts.

In the foreword to the professional text, *Hands Down, Speak Out*, Peter Johnston writes:

> *When children know how to think together well, they can solve more problems collaboratively than can groups who have not learned how to think together (Mercer, Wegerif, and Dawes 1999). But, that's not all. As they become more capable as a group, the individuals in the group become more capable than students who have not learned how to think together. This, alone, should place the ability to think together at the center of school curricula.*
>
> *(Omohundro Wedekind and Thompson 2020, xi)*

As a staff developer for twenty years and a classroom teacher, I can attest to Peter Johnston's words. Over and over, I have seen kids' comprehension, and thus their talk, deepen as the classroom community learns to talk together. What surprises me the most about "teaching talk" is that I don't think there is anything more joyful than watching kids have a hands-down conversation on their own. Once it gets going, it looks and feels like magic. I've had people watch the children in action and ask, "How did you get them to do that?"

The steps to teach students how to have a hands-down conversation are simple. However, the hard part comes when pitfalls arise, like when we begin a conversation and all the kids sit in complete silence. This thirty seconds of silence feels like an eternity. Or when all the kids speak at once and students start interrupting one another. My least favorite moment is when students continue to repeat what someone else said, and the conversation becomes circular. These are the hard parts.

But isn't lots of teaching muddling through the hard parts? Student-centered talk, including hands-down conversations, is no different. When learning doesn't go as I expect, I have to remind myself that if this were math, for instance, I wouldn't give up and say, "Oh, forget it. They just can't do math." When math gets hard, I muddle through. I revise and reteach. I have students model, and I coach as students complete the work. These are the same moves that lift the quality of students' talk.

When I continue to teach through the hard parts and remember that my students are only seven or eight years old, I can see their efforts and their confidence grow. I hope over time, hands-down conversations become one of your favorite parts of the day too. It is one of the moments that sustains me during those tricky times.

✔ The Steps of a Hands-Down Conversation

Let's focus on the hands-down conversations that happen after I read aloud a text. (Please note that hands-down conversations in different subject areas follow these same steps.) Sometimes the conversation happens right after we finish reading, while we are all gathered together on the carpet, but more often than not, the students capture their thinking in some way in the moment, and then, later on, we have a conversation. Let me show you the steps I generally follow. To help out, I have also included the language I sometimes use during each step. Please know that the language is only there as an example, as there are unlimited ways to bring this type of teaching to life. The best way to teach is to be your authentic self—there is no magic in what I say.

Step 1: Getting the Materials

All you need to start hands-down conversations with kids are some large pieces of paper, a few great texts that pique kids' interests (I'll give suggestions later in this chapter), a couple of packets of 3×4 sticky notes, and a pencil for each student.

The large paper can be chart paper, 8×14 copy paper, or a large sketchbook. The purpose of this paper is to capture student thinking, so anything large enough for this purpose will do. My personal preference is a large sketchbook. Each year, I purchase a large 18×24 art sketchbook to use as my whole-class notebook. I prefer to use a notebook so that I can refer back to previous conversations we've had. This notebook also makes it easy to see how the students' thinking has progressed through the school year.

After we have finished a read-aloud, I ask kids to pause and think on their own. I often ask, "What is your big thinking about this book? Let's write it down so we can talk about it together." Then I pass out sticky notes for the kids to use to capture their thinking. I like to use the 3×4 inch sticky notes with young learners so they have more room to write and draw. Later in the year, I have sticky notes available for kids to use during the read-aloud (instead of just after it), but I have found that having nothing in their hands helps students pay attention earlier in the school year. In Figure 4.2 you can see some early-in-school-year examples of second graders' sticky note recordings that they made after listening to a read-aloud of *Big Boys Cry* by Jonty Howley. I generally put a copy of the book cover on a page of our whole-class notebook and kids place their thinking around it.

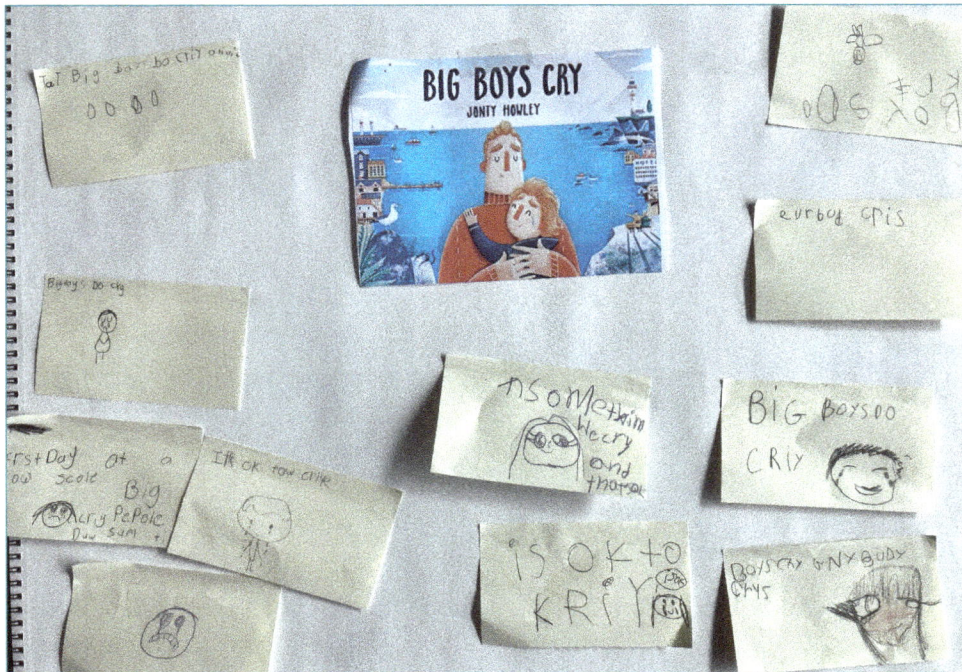

Figure 4.2
Early in the year, second graders record their thinking about our read-aloud, *Big Boys Cry*.

When I introduce the whole-class notebook and the sticky notes to readers, here is how that might sound:

> *Readers, this giant book is a special notebook that will hold lots of the thinking we do together this year. On each page, I will place a picture of a text we read or a video we watched. Then you will write or draw your thoughts about that text on a sticky note. After you are done, you will put it in this book so we can all see each other's big ideas. Later we will talk about our ideas in a hands-down conversation. I can't wait to read and hear your big ideas.*

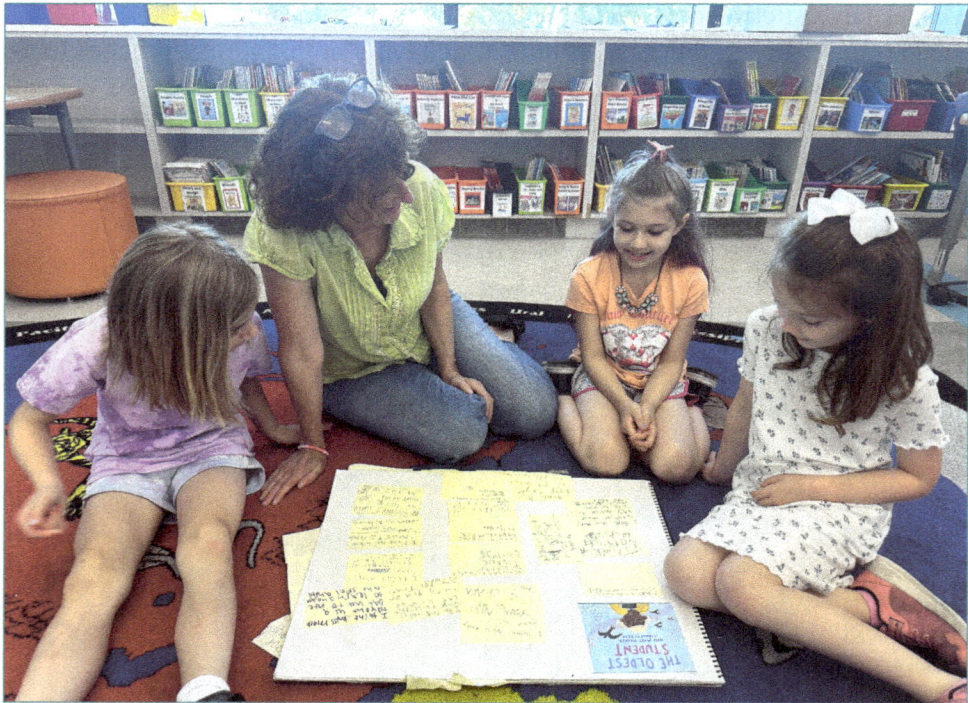

Figure 4.3
Students add their thinking to the whole-class notebook in preparation for a hands-down conversation.

Step 2: Reading the Text Aloud

When I read aloud, or when students watch a text on the screen, they sit next to a turn and talk partner. During read-aloud, I intentionally create heterogeneous partners, as it doesn't matter what levels of text complexity students read independently when I am reading the text aloud. What matters is that students feel comfortable speaking and listening with their partners.

TEACHER TIP

To set partners up for success, I teach students what to do when their partner is absent. We practice asking to join a group right near them by saying, "My partner is not here. May I join your conversation?" The other students know to respond, "Yes, absolutely," or, "We would love to have you."

Turn and talk partnerships change about every three or four weeks. I like to keep kids together for a little while as I notice their conversations generally deepen when they are together. When things are working well, I will often overhear children referring to something they discussed with their partner on a prior day or even comparing and contrasting texts together.

When a few partnerships are less successful, which typically happens whenever you group kids, I often sit in with that partnership to support their conversations. The bottom line is that there are no hard and fast rules for partnering students. Do what works for the kids in front of you.

Once kids are sitting on the carpet next to their partner, I read aloud, stopping at particularly interesting points in the text to ask students to turn and talk with their partners. If you were in my classroom the first time I introduced turn and talk, here is how it might sound:

> *Readers, let's gather and sit by our partners. I can't wait to hear your thoughts about this text. I'll read aloud and you will listen. When we get to some surprising or exciting parts, I'll ask you to turn and talk with your partner. This is a time when you might say, "I think. . . ." and tell your partner your thoughts about the character, the lessons characters might learn, or even something you notice about the words or the illustrations. Remember to take turns talking. If you speak first, ask your partner, "What do you think?" and then listen. When talking time is over, you will hear me reading again. This is your signal to turn right back and listen so we can read more. Let's try it.*

Step 3: Recording Your Thinking

As soon as I finish reading a text, students share their final thoughts with their partners. Then, they head off to a table to record their thinking. I've put sticky notes (one per person) on the tables so students can get right to work writing or drawing their biggest ideas about the book. This process only takes one to two minutes and I send kids off saying something like,

> *Now it is time to record your thinking. Think about your biggest idea about this book. Maybe you are thinking about the life lesson this book is teaching, or perhaps you are thinking about something a character learned. You might even be thinking about something you learned. Write or draw your idea, and when you are done, please place your sticky note in the whole-class notebook and sit at your rug spot again. Everyone will be done in a moment and our hands-down conversation will begin.*

As students bring their ideas on sticky notes over to the notebook, I often read them aloud or explain what the picture shows to give others, who may be having difficulty, some ideas for what to write. Their independence will come.

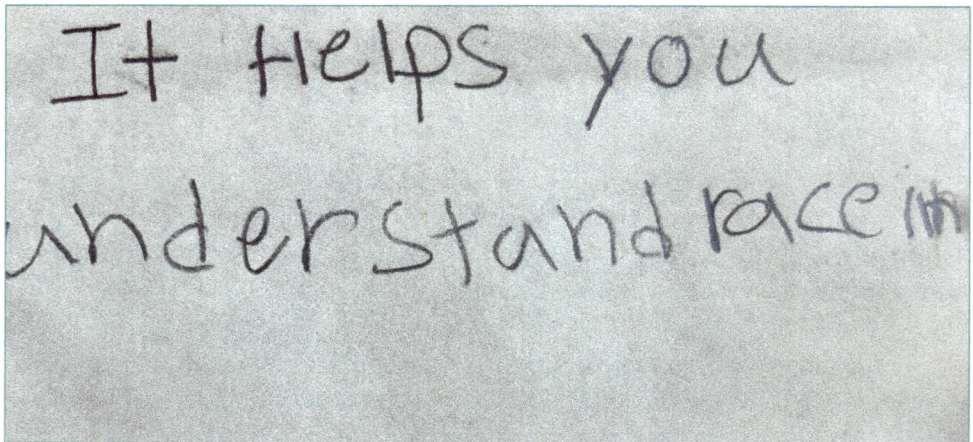

Figure 4.4
A student's response ("it helps you understand racism") after a read-aloud of *Not Quite Snow White* by Ashley Franklin.

But for now, I am teaching them how to engage in the process.

I want to emphasize that I *do not* have students record their thinking about every book I read aloud. Instead, I take my cues from the kids. I watch to see which books grab their interest and I act from there.

Step 4: Have a Hands-Down Conversation

Before the conversation begins, I introduce or review some helpful talking prompts. These prompts are listed on an anchor chart [Figure 4.5], and this chart is built throughout the year, adding possible talking prompts as students become more proficient with their conversational skills. At the beginning of the year, we start with three talking prompts:

- I think_____.
- [Child's name], I heard you say_____.
- [Child's name], what makes you think that?

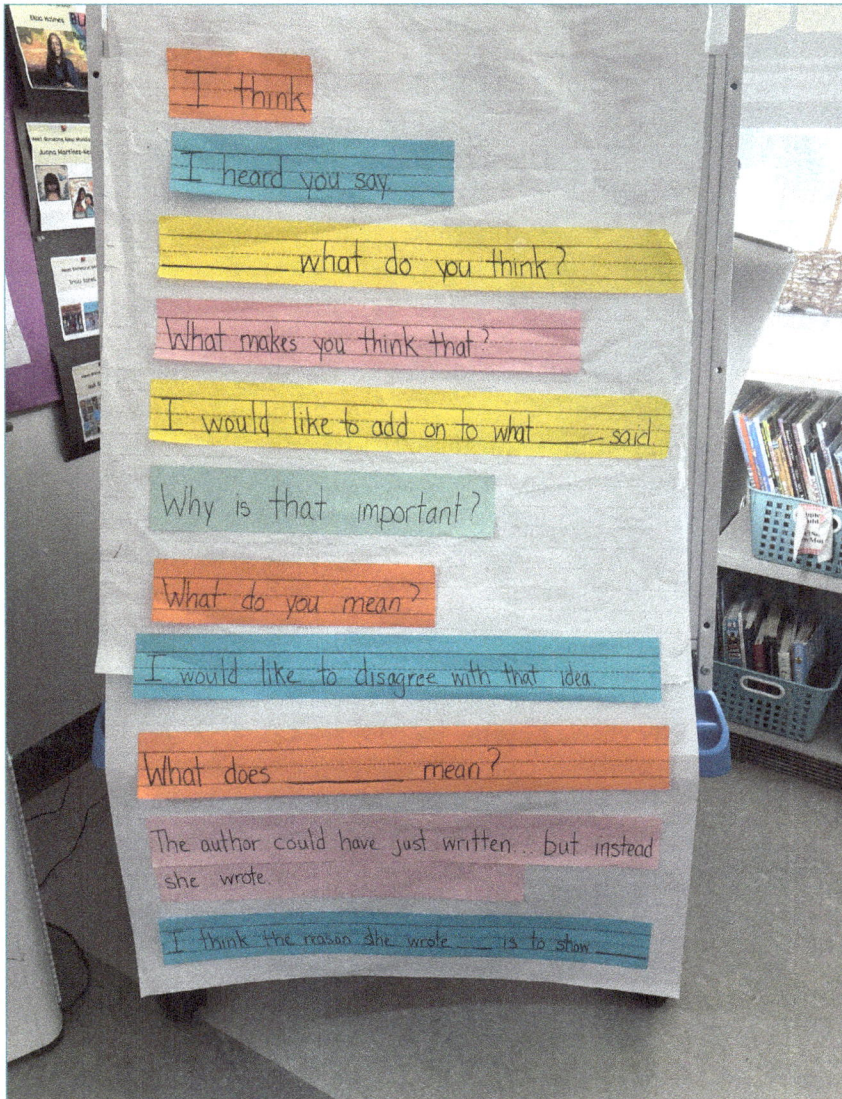

Figure 4.5
A talking prompt chart that was created over the course of the school year. As I introduce new teaching points, the chart grows.

As the weeks go on, and I notice that students use the language somewhat independently, I add more talking prompts. I choose new prompts to match what my students need and the literacy curriculum I teach. Once I've reviewed some talking prompts, we begin.

I say, "Let's remember, in a hands-down conversation, we look at the person who is speaking and then we listen and respond. We add our voices to the conversation, but we are also sometimes quiet to make sure we include everyone."

Then, six kids raise their hands and a few others call out, "Can I start?"—this always makes me laugh inside. I ask everyone to put their hands down. I assure them that one person will start talking, others will wait, and we will grow our thinking together. The most important thing they can do is listen to one another.

There is quiet for three seconds and then, nine times out of ten, three or four kids speak at once. I remain quiet because kids need to solve this problem on their own and they do. Generally, several students back down, and one shares their ideas. Then others chime in and we are on our way—not perfectly, but perfection is not the goal. Learning to notice more, listen, and deepen our thinking is what matters most.

The conversation continues for three to five minutes and for the most part, I sit in the circle quietly. During this time, I may give a head nod to a student to encourage them to speak or I take notes as they talk to capture parts of the conversation. My listening moves help me choose a teaching point for this moment or to teach later, and the notes I take will sometimes be part of an upcoming lesson.

✔ Listen, Notice, and Choose One Teaching Point

As I listen to the kids' conversation, teaching point after teaching point jumps into my mind. It often feels like there is so much to work on that I don't know where to begin. Depending on the day, I might notice that:

- Students speak over one another.
- Some students are silent while others monopolize the conversation.
- The entire group is silent, and no one speaks.
- Students are repeating ideas rather than building on what others say.

It is during these moments I need to remind myself that the children are rookies at hands-down conversations. All of the teaching points I see—awkward moments of silence, uncomfortable giggling, and even bursts of students talking over one another—are normal parts of the learning process.

Since this is all normal, it means there are many right next teaching steps. The teaching points are not completely linear and there isn't a list of steps. The art of conversation is nuanced and complex because there are so many pieces to it. It reminds me of teaching someone to ride a bike—you have to steer, balance, pedal, and pay attention to your surroundings simultaneously. The kids are giving hands-down conversations their best shot, and they just can't quite put it all together right now. Their conversational skills will grow as the school months pass, and yet they will still be young learners who will continue learning about the art of conversation throughout their lives. My job is to teach them a few moves to help them on their journey as conversationalists.

As I choose what to teach, I also keep in mind that I *want* students to love talking about texts. If I correct everything and don't ignore some behaviors, I end up over-teaching, over-correcting, and siphoning the joy out of the whole experience. Talking about books is supposed to be fun and I have to remind myself to keep it joyful. For the most part, I let the squirming happen, and don't let these sessions go on for very long (just a few minutes). Remember, this is a quick and frequent move. We want to end on a positive note.

As the kids talk, I put my energy into watching who is talking, who is listening, and what they are saying. I use a few note-taking tools to help me see patterns and choose future teaching points.

Note-Taking Tool 1—Scribe a Snippet of Conversation

One way I take notes is to scribe a snippet of the conversation. I write down (or try to write down) exactly what was said in a thirty-second time frame. I literally take my computer and type as students talk. Now, I do *not* capture everything they say, but even if I can capture the conversation of five or six speakers, I have enough information. My goal is to find patterns in the conversation and use this information to teach. Here is the snippet I typed as students had a hands-down conversation about the book *Knight Owl* by Christopher Denise.

> *I think the lesson in the book is to be kind.*
>
> *I think the lesson is to try to accomplish your dreams.*

I think the lesson is to be brave, even if you are a little scared.

You should always stand up for yourself, even if someone is bigger than you.

I heard you say that you should stand up for yourself even if someone is bigger than you, and I agree. In the story, Owl saw the enormous dragon and didn't run away.

Do you see how the students can identify a theme now? More often than not, I use the notes to highlight something they did well or point out a conversational move I want them to keep doing.

I also see in these notes that the conversation is repetitive, and students are not building ideas off of one another. I know I have to teach this, but I don't say this aloud when I am showing kids the notes, as I want this experience to be positive. Instead, I am more apt to point out a specific comment someone made that *added* to the conversation instead of repeating it, so they can all learn from this move. I think the line "I heard you say that you should stand up for yourself even if someone is bigger than you, and I agree. In the story, Owl saw the enormous dragon and didn't run away" is a great point to highlight. This student responded to another student's idea and supported their thinking with text evidence. Once students see the conversation written down and notice the conversational moves of others, they often try them out during the next hands-down conversation.

Note-Taking Tool 2—Keep Track of Who Speaks

I draw a circle on a blank piece of paper and put a number on the circle each time someone speaks [Figure 4.6]. The goal of this kind of note-taking is to help the students see who is talking and whose voice is missing from the conversation. When students see how often they speak, or remain silent, they adjust their actions in future conversations.

Now, I know this data collection is imperfect because I don't always catch every single time a student speaks on this record, but I like it that way. I don't want names around the circle because I want the kids to see general patterns and not search for their names. My point with this data display is for kids to notice that not everyone is speaking, and in order to have a more inclusive conversation it will mean that some children need to speak less and others need to speak more.

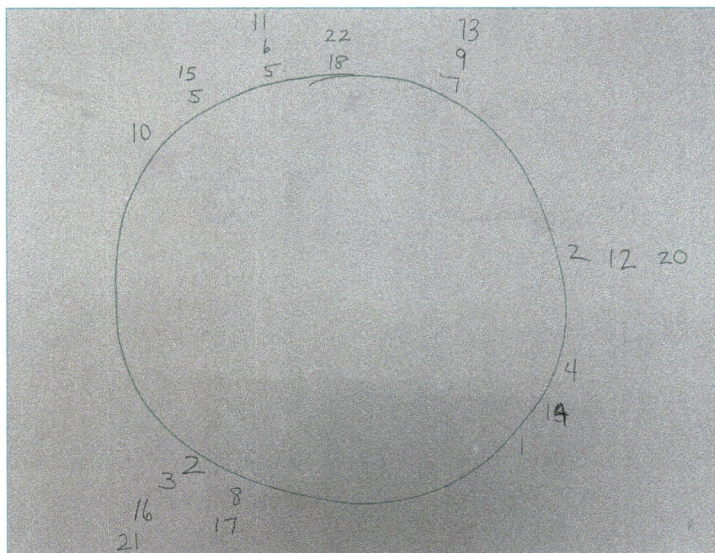

Figure 4.6
A sample recording of how the conversation moved around the circle during a hands-down conversation. The number one indicates where the conversation began, and the following numbers show how the conversation moved between the children. The numbers stacked on top of one another show that the same student spoke that many times.

In this data display, we can see that the conversation is mostly happening at the top and bottom of the circle and hardly anyone seated on the left side of the circle is speaking. When I show the circle to students, they can see this too, and this is a perfect opportunity for them to think about the number of times they speak up.

Note-Taking Tool 3—Ask the Kids

One piece of data I don't want to forget about is the kids' opinions and ideas. Hands-down conversations are *their* conversations, and they do know what is going well and what isn't working. Periodically, after a hands-down conversation, I ask the class to jot or draw on two sticky notes in response to these two questions:

- What is one thing that is going well during hands-down conversations?
- What are ways we can improve our hands-down conversations?

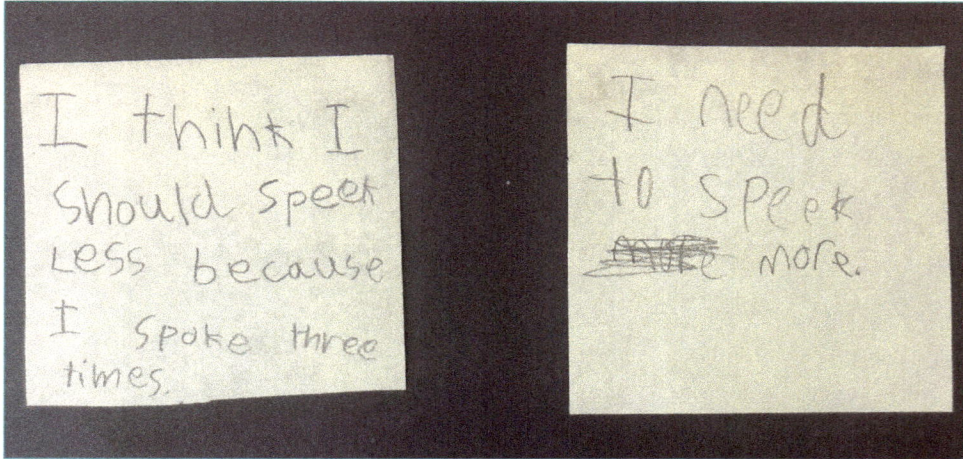

Figure 4.7
Two student reflections after seeing the data of how the conversation moved throughout the classroom.

When I read what students wrote on their sticky notes, I am often relieved because, for the most part, their observations align with my own. And, more often than not, someone in the class points out something I missed that I can add to my list of future teaching points.

I keep the kids' list of teaching points right at my fingertips because when students see their strengths and next steps, they own the learning, and now my future teaching can be about what they want to learn. I refer to their teaching points as I teach over the next few weeks so they know that their feedback matters.

These data-collection tools are messy and imperfect, but they are also manageable and helpful. I can collect this data while I am teaching and immediately put it to use. As you look at your data, please remember that with practice and teaching, your students' conversational skills will grow throughout the year. Yet, they will still have conversations like the five-, six-, seven-, or eight-year-olds they are. We can help our learners to think deeply about texts while simultaneously savoring the unexpected language and ideas that come out of children's mouths. These are the moments that make our teaching days so much fun.

✔ Possible Teaching Points for Hands-Down Conversations

While there are many productive teaching points for helping students grow as conversationalists, let's take a deeper look into a few important ones I teach frequently in my class.

Possible Teaching Point: Take Turns Talking

Yes, when kids have hands-down conversations, they interrupt each other, and some even monopolize the conversation. These things happen in adult conversations too, but somehow these problems seem more subtle when adults do it. With kids, the conversation screams, "*This isn't working!*"

When I teach kids about turn-taking in conversations, I begin with the feedback the students gave me about how hands-down conversations in the class are going. I pull it out and begin.

> *Thanks for sharing all the ways you think our hands-down conversations are working and possible next steps. I agree with what you wrote and drew about our strengths and next steps. I want to tell you something you might not know. When grown-ups have hands-down conversations, these same problems happen. Did you know that there are strategies we can try? Are you ready to try some new moves?*

Kids nod their heads in agreement, even though I don't think all of them are sure. But, nevertheless, I continue on and add new language to our anchor chart.

> *Today, let's talk about what to do when we all talk at the same time.*
>
> *When several kids all talk at the same time, we can try two moves:*
>
> *1. Stop talking for a moment and let someone else finish.*
> *2. Ask someone to speak. "[Child's name], what do you think?"*
>
> *Let's have a quick hands-down conversation about our favorite recess games. [Child's name], will you start us off? Now, instead of all jumping in to answer, let's try our two new moves, and remember if you spoke once, give space to let someone else have a turn.*

The conversation begins and is a tiny bit better. Beginning with a familiar topic gives kids some quick practice right at the moment. I write in my plan book to practice this move again when we talk about our latest read-aloud. Just like with everything else, change will take time.

Possible Teaching Point: Actively Participate and Encourage Others

Students who repeatedly speak during hands-down conversations and those who don't say a word are on opposite sides of the problem, but also have so much in common. When I teach this lesson, my goal is *not* to turn introverts into extroverts (goodness knows, we need self-reflective, quiet listeners in society), but I do want to help all children notice conversational patterns and make sure everyone feels they have a voice in the classroom.

The good news is that the whole-class notebook ensures that everyone has contributed their thinking through writing and drawing, so everyone has had input in one way. So now I want to help the group be more inclusive and notice whose voices need to be raised up.

> *Today I want to teach you some ways to make sure everyone has an opportunity to share their thinking during our hands-down conversations. The first step is to listen closely and notice your actions. Let's look at this data chart I collected last time we had a hands-down conversation [Figure 4.6]. Each number shows when someone spoke. The numbers go in order of how the conversation hopped from one person to the next. Take a look for a moment. What do you notice?*
>
> *Yes. I noticed the same thing. Some parts of our circle have lots of talking marks, and others have none. When we have conversations, we have to think about how many times we speak—zero times, once, twice, or even more. Then when we notice how much we're talking, we do something about it.*
>
> *For example, if you spoke once, twice, or even more, you will want to listen more and notice who hasn't spoken. When you realize whose voice we have not heard, you can say, "[Child's name], what do you think?"*
>
> *If you are someone who hasn't spoken, you might want to listen closely to the conversation and think, "What do I want to say? Could I find a way to share my idea or get someone else to say more about their idea?" One way to start is to say another child's name and then ask a question or say your idea.*
>
> * *[Child's name], can you say more about _____?*
> * *[Child's name], I heard you say _____.*
> * *I would like to add on to what [child's name] said. I also think _____.*

Now we begin our conversation, and we end by highlighting what the group did well. After a few more conversations have happened, I will take notes again, and once more we will look for patterns as a class.

Possible Teaching Point: Be Patient with Silence

Awkward is the word that comes to mind when I think about how it feels when the whole class sits silently, uncomfortably staring at each other and saying nothing during a hands-down conversation. It is then that the giggling and the squirming can take over, and you can just see the whole thing deteriorate before your eyes.

It is okay if it does. I can move on and try again later. I can restart or I can teach. Not knowing what to say or how to act when the teacher isn't leading the group can feel uncomfortable, and this is one opportunity to teach that silence can be helpful.

> *Sometimes when we have hands-down conversations it gets quiet. When that happens there is something I want you to remember. I want you to remember that thinking takes time, and when we sit quietly, we can think and our classmates can think too.*
>
> *When everyone is quiet, you can use that time to ask yourself, "What has someone else said that made me think? Why is what _____ said important? What am I thinking now?" You can also use that time to think more about the topic or text we are talking about or ask a question about what others have said.*
>
> *Once you have an idea or a question, you have to decide whether you have spoken quite a bit and you should give space for others to speak, or you should share. Let's practice by having a hands-down conversation about our hands-down conversations. What are your thoughts about the quiet during hands-down conversations?*

With all of these teaching points, I try to normalize the problem for students. Then, I take a deep breath, validate the problem, and lean in a bit. When we lean into the hard parts, we are helping our kids learn that their voice matters and so do the voices of others.

✔ Choosing Texts for Hands-Down Conversations

When I use texts for hands-down conversations, I often integrate texts from other parts of the curriculum. Sometimes I choose a picture book biography about a scientist, engineer, artist, or mathematician connected to the content we are studying. Other times, I choose texts that are set in places around the world to enhance our geography unit of study. I try to choose a few texts that go together—the same genre, similar theme, or similar content—so children can make connections across texts and deepen their understanding.

Fluency Texts That Do Double Duty

The texts, songs, poems, and scripts for fluency instruction listed in Chapter 3 are one source for texts to talk about. I don't have hands-down conversations about all of these texts. Instead, when one of these texts resonates with kids, brings up points about justice and equity, lets them ponder new ideas or perspectives, or lends itself to discussing central themes, I choose it. If it doesn't, the poem, song, or script is just used during fluency practice.

Picture Book Biographies

Another resource for texts for hands-down conversations are picture book biographies and video interviews that I use to introduce students to influential people. (For more on this practice, see Chapter 5.) These texts are almost always strong choices for hands-down conversations. I want the kids to have opportunities to talk about the people they meet through these books so they can discuss the commonalities among all people, and learn about people's struggles, and how they overcame them. These books show people in leadership moments and how they persevered to make their voices heard, stood up for their beliefs despite the many obstacles in their way, and, in the end, learned to believe in themselves.

Short Videos

There are so many three- to five-minute videos that inspire kids to engage in meaningful conversations. Here are a few of my tried and true resources. These links will lead you to many others.

Learn with Liz (YouTube Channel)

These social-emotional videos are clever, funny and teach topics to help our class become a joyful learning community. My two favorite videos are *The Circle of Control* and *Flipping Your Lid*. In *The Circle of Control*, Liz gives kids strategies for understanding what they have the power to change and what they can choose to ignore from other people. In *Flipping Your Lid*, kids learn some important information about their brains and strategies to accept and manage their big feelings. After the children watch these videos, I ask them to jot or draw in response to the question, "What did you learn that you think is important for helping us create a joyful classroom community?" Kids have lots to say about these topics and often ask if we can watch the video again.

Pixar Shorts for Kids

These Pixar short films are filled with big ideas that are accessible to young kids and have profound messages that kids have lots to say about. After watching *The Present*, *For the Birds*, and *Piper* on different occasions, students had deep discussions about perseverance, thinking before you act, and how to resist making judgments about others based on the way someone looks. I rely on these to help students build inferential thinking skills about themes as well as teach life lessons about perspective-taking and self-determination.

LifeVest Inside (YouTube Channel)

After watching the video *The Kindness Boomerang*, my students asked to see it again and again. This video sparked several conversations about how we can support one another to lift everyone up. Sometimes we rewatched this video before a hands-down conversation focused on being a strong writing partner. Other times, after watching *The Kindness Boomerang*, the kids explored how they could support one another in a noisy and chaotic cafeteria.

Looking back, I see how much joy these videos brought into the classroom. They became the basis for many of our inside jokes and even launched a whole-class discussion about a name for our class. The class unanimously voted to be called The Kindness Crew.

✔ A Literacy Leadership Moment for Sam

One of our hands-down conversations this spring was about the text *How Do You Spell Unfair?: MacNolia Cox and the National Spelling Bee*, written by Carole Boston Weatherford and illustrated by Frank Morrison. This nonfiction picture book is about MacNolia Cox, an eighth grader who was cheated out of a first-place win by judges of the 1936 National Spelling Bee. As I closed the book, Sam looked at me and declared, "We need to have a hands-down conversation about that book. That was so unfair, and I can't believe that happened to MacNolia."

"Great idea, Sam. Let's jot down our big ideas about *How Do You Spell Unfair?* and then talk." Each student grabbed a sticky note at their table and began writing.

As students wrote, I grabbed the whole-class notebook and divided a page into four boxes and labeled the boxes—Plot (what happened in the story), Character Feelings (how a character felt), Theme (a lesson the story teaches), and Other Big Ideas. Then, as the students came over with their sticky note, I asked them to place their note in the quadrant that best matched the type of thinking they did. After the sticky notes were organized, I asked, "What do you notice about the ways we thought about this book?"

The room erupted into conversation, and it became evidently clear that most kids wanted to talk about the injustice and MacNolia's feelings. Sam launched the discussion, "I want to know what we would do if MacNolia were in our class."

I passed him the text and he held up a picture of the three judges choosing the final word for MacNolia to spell. "The white judges gave her a word that wasn't on the spelling bee list and MacNolia lost. That is cheating and that is racism. If MacNolia was in our class, we could stand by MacNolia and tell those judges they are wrong."

The conversation in the class continued and Sam's question was the catalyst for a robust conversation. Another literacy leadership moment for Sam.

5

Quick and Frequent Moves to Help Readers Meet Role Models

At the end of one school day. Jory's dad stopped me in the pickup line and asked, "Jory's reading will be fine. It will come, right?"

In this moment in the front of the school, with families and students chaotically swarming around, I answered back. (I know what you are thinking—big mistake. What a rookie move to answer him at that moment, and what I said wasn't the best either.) "Children do learn on different timelines, but Jory will need to work very hard for it. Let's set up a time to talk."

Once the words were out of my mouth, I saw the panic in his eyes, and I couldn't take them back. I don't know what I was thinking. Clearly, I wasn't.

I know this panic firsthand. I raised a child who didn't come to reading easily. I know this fear—the fear as you watch your child's self-esteem shrivel up each time they see a friend carrying a chapter book. The worry each time their friend confidently reads aloud the cards for a board game and your child lowers their head. And the outright punch in the gut when a parent tells you her kid stayed up all night reading. "I just can't get him to stop reading."

Jory's dad's comment hit personal heartstrings, and I misstepped. I set up a meeting immediately and apologized for answering him in the school parking lot. I still couldn't take it back.

As I thought about that mistake for days (and weeks), what bothered me was the myth that reading will "just come." Those words, "just come," are unhelpful when we talk about learning. Learning to read isn't like a sunset that appears in the sky each evening. For some, learning to read is just plain hard, and when kids think, "This should be easy for me," they equate ease of learning to read with smartness. And thus, when learning is hard they think, "I'm not smart." The bottom line is that many (if not most) children will have to do hard things in their lives, and for some kids, learning to read will be one of them.

Kids whose learning journeys are more straightforward right now also need to learn that they can do hard things. We don't want them to believe that, because reading may come to them with less effort, they are better, smarter, or more worthy than others. We all need perseverance, empathy, and self-reflection in our toolkits to face the challenges that will come. Quick and frequent practice is one tool I want learners to know they always have by their side. When they want to overcome something difficult, pursue a passion, or anything in between, they can make a plan with short bursts of practice to make progress.

Figure 5.1
I wrote a part of this chapter sitting outside a hospital emergency room as a friend dealt with a health crisis. This is the poster I see through the window.

✔ Meet Someone New as a Quick and Frequent Practice

The quick and frequent move this chapter focuses on is sharing the journeys of all different kinds of people so kids can learn a bit about the role of practice in people's lives. When students know about the learning journeys of others, their stories can be seeds of inspiration for kids' own learning processes. They see the "behind the curtain" process behind accomplishments, and the role of practice in these accomplishments.

Sharing these stories about other people's lives is a quick and frequent move that I call "Meet Someone New" in my classroom. It takes only ten to fifteen minutes each week during morning meetings or read-aloud time, but what kids learn about the diverse world around them and perseverance is invaluable. As Rudine Sims Bishop writes,

> *Books are sometimes windows, offering views of worlds that may be real or imagined, familiar or strange. These windows are also sliding glass doors and readers have only to walk through in imagination to become part of whatever world has been created or recreated by the author. When lighting conditions are just right, however, a window can also be a mirror. Literature transforms human experience and reflects it back as part of the larger human experience.*
>
> *(1990, ix)*

Through the pages of a book, stories of perseverance, determination, and self-worth come to life, and students meet people who can be windows, mirrors, and sliding glass doors for them. The stories of other people open up classroom conversations that dismantle the notion that some people are "smart" and others are "not as smart." Instead, students see people from all walks of life doing hard things and accomplishing greatness. During hands-down conversations, students discuss and ask questions about the people they "meet." They get to consider the obstacles and challenges people face, and the paths they take to reach their goals.

✔ Getting Started with Meet Someone New

Thanks to Melissa Quimby, and her article, "Meet Someone New Monday: Using Picture Book Biographies to Bring Marginalized Voices into the Classroom," I learned an engaging way to introduce students to new people regularly (2024). In her article, Quimby shares how she chooses picture book biographies and shows a short video snippet about the person, or a topic related to what this person has accomplished.

As soon as I heard about this idea, I was excited to see how this initiative could help children deepen their understanding of what persistence and perseverance look and sound like. No matter whether I introduce students to an author, artist, scientist, teacher, member of the military, or caregiver, we "meet" people who have done hard things and learn how practice has had a role in their journey.

✔ Planning for Meet Someone New

To begin, I use the Harvard Heritage and Awareness Calendar as a place to start (Harvard Office for Equity, Diversity, Inclusion and Belonging 2024). I do not limit who I introduce students to each month by a particular heritage, but do I use this guide to help me be more intentional about the breadth of people I choose.

To find picture book biographies that will excite and inspire my students, I search websites and blogs such as the ALA Youth Media Awards, Jillian Heise's #ClassroomBookADay initiative, and Choice Literacy. When choosing people, I think about the curriculum I am teaching, what students are passionate about, and where we live. For example, when artist and illustrator Ekua Holmes had an art exhibit at the Museum of Fine Arts here in Boston, I launched Meet Someone New with her as she lives just a few miles away from my students.

Since the children in my classroom all have a family member in the military, I also introduced them to Raye Montague, a brilliant mathematician who worked for the Navy. We learned about Raye Montague's life through the book *The Girl with a Mind for Math*. This book gave kids a chance to meet someone who had a passion for a skill we were learning (math), challenged stereotypes around what mathematicians look like, and highlighted a military hero.

As I get to know my students, I find people for Meet Someone New with similar interests as them. One year, I had several kids who loved sports. This was a perfect opportunity for our class to meet Shaquille O'Neal as he is the author of the *Little Shaq* series they might choose to read during the year.

One person I introduced early in the year is Mary Walker. In the picture book *The Oldest Student: How Mary Walker Learned to Read*, written by Rita Lorraine Hubbard and illustrated by Oge Mora, kids learn how Mary's life spanned from the Civil War through the 1960s civil rights movement. Mary learned to read at age 116. Each year I continue to add stories of people who had to persevere to learn to read such as Dav Pilkey, Albert Einstein, and Hudson Talbott.

After showing students a snippet of an interview with *Dog Man* and *Captain Underpants* creator Dav Pilkey, I heard Jory tell another student, "I am just like Dav Pilkey. We both had a hard time learning to read and we are both creative."

Another student smiled at Jory and declared, "I love listening to the stories you write at writing workshop." This interaction just warmed my heart. Jory saw a commonality with someone else and embraced it rather than trying to hide what is hard for her. She knows that, just like Dav Pilkey, her skills will grow and practice will help get her there.

I also introduce students to many children's book authors and illustrators through Meet Someone New. Grace Lin, Kat Zhang, Bryan Collier, Juana Martinez-Neal, Kwame Alexander, and Traci Sorell are just a few of the people we study. These are some of the authors and illustrators whose picture books I use as demonstration and mentor texts during reading and writing workshop throughout the year. As we enjoy the books they make, we also get to know these illustrators and authors as people, understand their creative processes, and learn about their lives.

Kids also love learning about youth who are making positive impacts in the world. Marley Dias, Greta Thunberg, and Olivia Bouler are three youth activists who are featured in picture books. But I don't limit the choices of people to just those who have a picture book written about them. For example, we recently read excerpts from an article called "5 Young Environmental Activists Making a Difference in Climate Change" (The One UN Climate Change Learning Partnership 2024). These youth saw a problem and are doing something about it. Isn't that what we want for students?

I've witnessed firsthand how Meet Someone New sparks ideas in kids and lets them know that they have the power to solve problems. One day, during reading workshop, Sam approached me, visibly upset. With an informational book about wolves in his hand, he said, "Mrs. Mulligan, did you know that people are killing wolves? We've got to stop this!" His passion launched him on an independent project to do more research and present his findings to other kids. He went to the library, found books he could read on the topic, and listened to read-alouds on the Epic! website. After a few days, he said, "Mrs. Mulligan, everyone needs to know about this so this killing will stop." Then he took that new knowledge and created a poster board of his findings and presented it to the classes at the grade level.

Sam saw a problem, made a plan, and took steps to make an impact. The poster board he created hung in the school library all year. His work was small, but we never know what kids will do in the future once they have the agency to make changes.

✔ Creating a Meet Someone New Slide Deck

To make the Meet Someone New project manageable, it needs to stay in the quick and frequent realm—ten to fifteen minutes a week. I create a slide for each person we learn about so that what I need is all in one place. The slide holds some basic information—a photo of the person (which I often get from their website), a picture of the picture book biography (taken from the publisher's website), and links to interviews or video clips about the person.

I don't have all of the slides created at the beginning of the school year. Instead, I add people as the year progresses once I learn more about my students' interests and passions. Having the structure for the slides helps to keep the work manageable but my teaching responsive. In my mind, I think, "I'll do Meet Someone New two or three times a month, and the slides will have this structure [Figure 5.2]. Then, all I have to do is choose people, and the curriculum evolves as I get to know my kids."

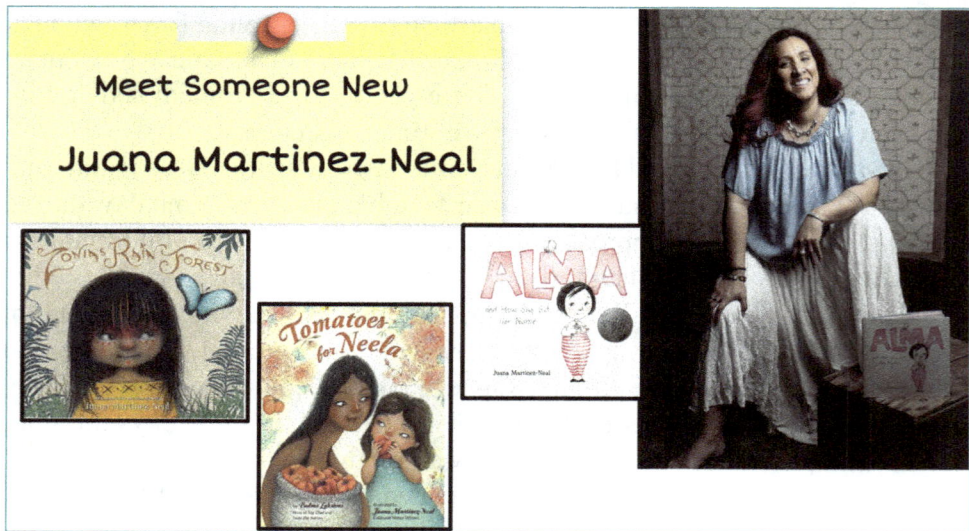

Figure 5.2
A sample slide for the author, Juana Martinez-Neal. In this slide, I added the books we will read aloud and links to a video of Juana reading one of her books on YouTube.

A note of caution: be careful to use links that the author and the picture book publisher have approved. Many videos of people reading children's books on YouTube violate copyright law.

✔ Introducing Students to Meet Someone New

More often than not, Meet Someone New happens in five- to ten-minute chunks of time over a few days—just like most quick and frequent moves. First, we read a book or watch a short video clip about the person. If the text or video is longer, we read/watch it over several sessions. I take my cue from the students and don't rush the process. When there is high interest, I reread a section of the book or rewatch a video snippet on another day. I intentionally weave this work throughout morning meeting, whole-class minilessons, and read-aloud, so that students can digest and retain information about the person. When I give some space and time between our discussions, I can listen to what piques students' interests and adjust my teaching. Kids also have time to make connections between what they are learning and the people they are meeting.

After introducing a new person, I print two copies of the slide. One copy hangs in the classroom so students can refer to it all year [Figure 5.3].

When pictures of the slides are up in the room, and the picture book biographies are available, students reference them during discussions. They often discuss similarities among people we meet, and I often find children exploring these books with peers during free moments.

The second slide copy goes into our whole-class notebook so we can have a hands-down conversation (see Chapter 4) about this person. When kids get to share their ideas about the people we meet, they discuss the patterns of injustice that are so apparent in these stories and the perseverance it took to overcome obstacles.

✔ Expanding Meet Someone New to Members of Our Community

The Meet Someone New project is also one way kids meet people in the school community. Custodians, each other's family members and caregivers, cafeteria workers, administrators, front office personnel, and the school nurse all have stories of perseverance to share.

Figure 5.3
Our Meet Someone New slides hang on the classroom door so students can refer back to them all year long.

At the beginning of the school year, I asked community members to come into the classroom and share a two- to three-minute story about the role of practice in their lives and how it helped them to accomplish something. Through this process, we learned things that we would never know from daily interactions with these people such as:

- The custodian is a fiction writer who sets aside time in his schedule before he comes to work to write each day.
- The special education teacher taught herself to crochet this summer. She purposefully began with short and easy projects—making mini crochet cacti. She loved the end products and making something small built her confidence and her skills.
- The cafeteria worker taught herself how to play the ukulele by watching lessons online and making time to practice each evening.

These short but frequent discussions of ways all different people in the world practice help kids understand that practicing something is "normal." Mastery does not come all at once. Instead, children come to understand that learning something new or accomplishing a goal comes first from a want, a need, a goal, or a desire, and then people make plans to practice frequently. All the people we meet had setbacks, but they also tried, when possible, to achieve some short-term successes on their way to longer-term goals.

These Meet Someone New discussions also help children understand the "why" behind the practice we do in class, and help them set their own practice goals. Instead of assignments and activities solely coming from me, students now see that they have a voice in the work they do at school, and that they can make quick and frequent plans to achieve their goals.

✔ Now It's the Kids' Turn: Celebrating Practice

After we've explored how others accomplish goals, it is time to turn this into a self-reflective practice. When I say that students "notice their practice," these are almost always small steps a child takes—not momentous achievements. For example, a child might share about how they didn't give up on a tricky word and instead reached for their mini sound book. Or a child might choose to revise a particular part of their fiction story after a partner gave them feedback about an unclear part. It is noticing these daily choices that add up to significant accomplishments.

When I set up the classroom, I create space on the walls for students to capture and document the efforts learners make to accomplish their goals. I cover the main bulletin board and some wall space with 11×14-inch matte frames (one per student). The frames are empty except for a student's name inside it [Figure 5.4].

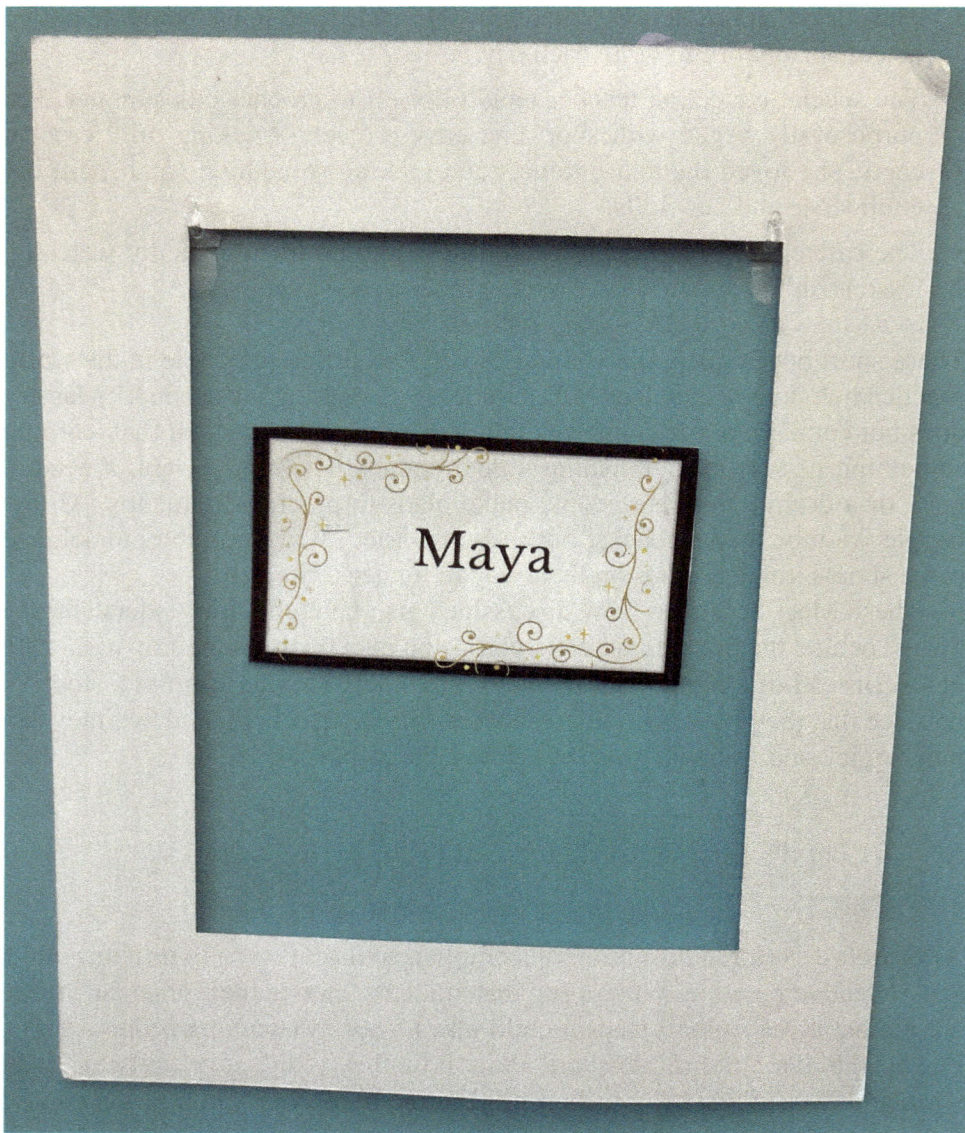

Figure 5.4
When the children enter the classroom on the first day of school, they see their name inside a blank frame.

Then, over the first few weeks of school, the children decorate their frames. The first step is to cover the white matte frame with a tissue paper collage. Then, after it dries, children spend moments over the next several weeks (and throughout the school year) decorating the actual frame with images, drawings, and words that represent themselves—what they enjoy, the important people in their lives, their beliefs, and even their hopes. The words and pictures they add to their identity frames help us learn about each other during these first few weeks of school and beyond [Figure 5.5].

Figure 5.5
A student's frame shows a photo of him showcasing his successful performance of a Reader's Theater play.

These frames become the places that hold 8×10 inch photos of kids show-casing proud practice moments. For example, last week in Sam's frame there was a picture of him holding up a *Pedro* book because each day that week he read a chapter until he completed the book. Then in Maya's frame is a picture of her with the recently published book she wrote. When I took the picture, she opened the book to a page where she worked hard to fix up her spelling, so she could highlight this accomplishment. These images of kids practicing are proudly displayed all over the room, and they are one way we, as a classroom community, celebrate hard work and practice.

We begin this self-reflection process during the first months of school each Friday morning. Each Friday, I ask students to find an item that represents a moment in which they've persevered. It might be a book, a writing piece, a math activity, an art project, an entry in their science journal, or anything else. Once they find this item, they bring it to our meeting area. Then students sit in small groups and tell each other the small steps they took to learn something new and accomplish their goals. As kids share, I encourage them to remember the small steps they took to practice and highlight those for others in their group. I want students to focus on the process of learning, rather than simply celebrating the end product. It's the journey that matters, as much as the destination.

To scaffold these hands-down small-group conversations, I offer different ways students can share their ideas and ways for listeners to respond thoughtfully. These talking prompts provide a useful support for some while others speak more off the cuff.

What to say when you share:

- I worked hard when I…
- At first, I tried… Then I did…
- This is important to me because…
- To practice more, I will…

Ways to respond when others share:

- Congratulations on learning…
- I noticed you…
- Can you tell me more about…
- What part was the trickiest?

- What part makes you the proudest?
- Can you show me how to…
- What did you do to practice?

What I marvel at through this process is the stories behind their selections. Students share their efforts to problem-solve and try again or a moment when they showed vulnerability as a learner. These conversations help me too, as often I didn't realize the thought process behind the work a student completed. Now I know a bit more about these students.

As I listen to the conversations, I hear these snippets:

- "On this page in my math journal, I had to redo the first four problems. At first, I didn't understand, but now I do."
- "I read this book three times so I could make my reading sound like I was talking."
- "At first, I got frustrated when I drew a dog in my story. But I asked Sally to show me how she does it, and then I tried again."

As the groups finish talking, I take a photo (with the class iPad) of each child holding up their artifact. Then, when I have a free moment, or after school, I print out 8×10 photos. The students take their old photo out of their frame, put it in a thin binder of clear plastic sleeves, and put up the new picture. This thin binder is one way the kids document their growth over time, and they love looking at these photos and sharing them with their families. It is all about the process of learning, and these photos are one way to capture it.

As the year progresses, this process of taking photos becomes more organic. Throughout the week, students will bring work up to me and ask, "I worked so hard on this. Can you take a picture?" Or even better, a student will take selfies and airdrop them to me. Then, during a prep period, I can print them out. What is tricky about this process isn't the number of photos coming my way—that wanes with time—it is more about making sure all students notice their steps along their learning journey. To make sure I don't miss anyone, I put in my plan book a time each month to have the students all bring an artifact to morning meeting that represents some practice they have done. This way, I am sure to celebrate everyone.

Through this simple act of taking photos, I hope students learn that learning does not "just come." It is through their effort that small changes lead

to big ones. Just like the people they meet through our Meet Someone New routine, the true wisdom is in the story of the journey. The more we give space and time for children to name and notice the practice they initiate, the small steps they take, the more they will keep doing them. I hope this process gives all children knowledge and perspective about the ups and downs of learning, but I especially hope it inspires students like Jory, Maya, and Sam to persevere through the hard parts. All of our students have so much to offer the world; it is up to us to give them mirrors so they can see it.

6

Quick and Frequent Moves to Help Readers Lead

It is the fall of 2020, and I am reentering the classroom as a second-grade teacher after being a literacy consultant for more than twenty years. The kids and I are all in masks and sitting six feet apart from one another. I'm trying to teach math and, after focusing solely on literacy for decades, I am a definite rookie. Teaching math again feels challenging. Before each math lesson, I practice. I practice the games that are a part of the curriculum, and I honestly have to give myself a little pep talk. "I've got this. I know what I am doing."

Then I start to teach. But just a little way into the lesson, things go awry; the way you record the rolls of the dice and where students place the answer on the recording sheet becomes muddled in my head. Let's just say my directions are less than clear and the lesson does not go as well as planned. My lesson was unclear because I didn't know enough about what I was teaching. I only thought I did. Now I need to step back, learn more, and then, in another moment, reteach that concept.

The next day I have an opportunity to explain my learning missteps to the kids, which sounds a bit like this, "Yesterday I tried to teach you a game that will help you think about how combinations of ten can help you solve even trickier problems. I thought I understood and was ready to teach it to you, but when I tried to explain it I realized that I didn't understand it enough myself. I did some more learning on my own and I would like to reteach the game to you. What are your thoughts about redoing yesterday's lesson?" Thank goodness children are forgiving. They welcome my reteaching and give me another chance to do better.

Missteps like this one have helped me realize that our own past struggles to learn something offer us advantages when we try to teach someone else later. Since I had to work hard to figure something out, I understand the ins and outs of the strategy or concept. I know what it looks and feels like to be confused because I have experienced it firsthand. And now I also understand how to move beyond these misunderstandings, by increasing my own practice.

This psychological power of teaching others, the protégé effect, was introduced by Jean-Pol Martin (1985). The protégé effect describes how both preparing to teach others and actually teaching others helps you learn the information yourself. Dr. Itamar Shatz (2024) describes the benefits of the protégé effect:

- Increased metacognitive processing, which makes people more actively aware of their learning process.
- Increased use of effective learning strategies, such as organizing the material and seeking out key pieces of information.
- Increased motivation to learn, since people will often make a greater effort to learn for those that they will teach than they do for themselves.
- Increased feelings of competence and autonomy, by encouraging people to view themselves as playing the role of a teacher, rather than that of the student.

The protégé effect explains why finding opportunities to shift roles and let kids do some of the teaching is another small move with big impacts. And like many of the other quick and frequent practice moves in this book, it only takes a few minutes.

In each of our classrooms, there are students who receive lots of additional support. They often work with a teacher and participate in lots of individualized and small-group instruction. Don't get me wrong. So much of what I have written in this book is about providing focused instruction to kids who need it. Yet, at the same time, I worry about the unintended messages all of the efforts to provide intensive instruction may send to a young learner—"You are not as competent as others" or "You need help." While these worries don't stop me from teaching students what they need to learn, they do make me reflect on the opportunities these students have to be leaders as well. Creating literacy leadership moments allows children to be helpers instead of always the ones receiving help.

So I plan for these times when I can flip the student/teacher relationship on its head. I make space for opportunities for students to be the ones in charge as they expand their own understanding while also teaching a concept to someone else—literacy leadership moments.

✔ Creating Literacy Leadership Moments: Teaching Through Video

Since I want children to teach others frequently, I have to keep these teaching opportunities manageable. One of the easiest ways students can teach is through video. My students use the journal feature on Seesaw to create teaching videos to share with their classmates and their families. Students create videos about all kinds of skills and concepts—how to solve a tricky word, how to find the central message in a text, and even how to write and add small actions or dialogue to their stories.

Since I must approve these videos through the Seesaw app before anyone else can see them, I get to watch them first. I love watching students teach because it gives me so much insight into what they understand and what are possible next steps for their learning. As I watch, I sit with my conferring notebook by my side so I can capture any teaching points I notice. Then I leave each student a voice comment through the app, sharing what I noticed about their teaching.

A bonus of these videos is that families get to see them too and can listen to my comments. They can also write back to their child on Seesaw. I love how this tool helps families get a glimpse into the classroom. Then I can (with student permission) show the video in class and incorporate students' teaching videos into my whole-class and small-group instruction.

✔ Creating Literacy Leadership Moments: The Student Writing Teacher

During writing workshop, on the day before spring break, Sam looks at me and asks, "Since I finished my traditional tale yesterday, could I help other kids finish their traditional tales today instead of starting something new?"

I pause for a moment and consider this idea. It is true. I had conferred with him several times on his piece and he had just created a video on Seesaw to share his writing. It is also the Friday before spring break, so I understand why

Sam doesn't want to begin a new piece. I quickly respond, "Thanks, Sam. When you help other writers, please notice something they are doing well and tell them. Writers need lots of encouragement."

Sam sets off, and I begin working with other kids. Honestly, I am so preoccupied with supporting the students who need to finish their traditional tales that I don't think much more about it for a few minutes. Then out of the corner of my eye, I see Sam grabbing his chair and pulling up alongside other children, and I listen in.

"I want to make my character talk. What do you think she should say?"

"What if your character said, _____?" Sam asks, giving a suggestion of dialogue.

A student at another table asks for support, "I want to make sure my writing makes sense. Can you listen to this part?"

Sam reads that student's writing and responds, "This part makes sense, but you need to explain what is happening right here."

Then Maya asks for some spelling help, "I want to spell the word *adventure*, but it is tricky."

Sam says, "Can you clap the syllables in that word? Don't forget, every syllable has a vowel."

At this point, I stop conferring and just observe Sam's interactions. Other kids call out, "Sam, can you come to me next?" They are eager to share their writing and talk about what they are trying to do—a literacy leadership moment for Sam.

As I watch, I think back to all the writing retreats I've attended. As a writer, I learn a lot from listening to other people's writing. Listening to others helps me find new topic ideas, learn new craft moves, and inspires me to write more. Sam's idea of having a "student writing teacher" was brilliant and now all I needed to do was systematize it so everyone could have this leadership opportunity.

A Daily Student Writing Teacher—Putting Kids in Charge

To keep the system simple, I hang a clipboard with a list of class names in the writing center. I attach a clothespin to the class list to track who the student writing teacher is for the writing period. At the end of each writing period, the student writing teacher moves the clip to the next student's name and lets them know that it will be their turn to teach others tomorrow. If a student says that they would rather not be the student writing teacher for the day, that is just fine. We typically skip them for that day and then the next person on the list has their turn the following day. Sometimes, students are so invested in their own writing project that they don't want to leave it for a day. I leave this choice to them.

Tools for the Student Writing Teacher

Now that we have a system to take turns, I need to systematize how students know who to work with each day. I don't want the hum of a productive writing workshop interrupted with calls of, "Come work with me!" I also don't want some children to have many opportunities to work with a peer and others to have very few. All kids should have access to peer support, as well as the right to say, "Thanks—I'm all set today. I don't need a conference."

To help everything run smoothly, the student writing teacher carries a class list and simply puts an X next to a name once they finish conferring with a particular student. Then they move to the next student on the list. This way everyone gets equal access to the student writing teacher and the next student writing teacher knows just where to pick up tomorrow.

Who is in our class?

Jory
Maya
Michael
Nielson
Sam

Figure 6.1
A partial list of students so you can see how simple the list is.

I do not tell the student writing teacher how many children to see in a day. If they meet with two students, listen to their writing, and then get back to work—that is great. If they move from student to student and meet with six or seven other students, that works too. The goal is for students to learn from what others are doing and to think metacognitively about the writing process. I can always add parameters if I need to, but for now, I keep it open-ended.

Besides the class list [Figure 6.1], a pencil, and a small chair to carry around the room, the student writing teacher doesn't need any other physical materials. If they want extra paper, sticky notes, or a mentor text, those are all accessible in the writing area to take at any time. And while the student writing teacher doesn't need a lot of physical tools to get started, I do take time to teach the entire class what to say to their peers to begin a writing conference as well as some ways writers can ask for feedback or support.

The first questions we start with are openers to begin a conference. Phrases such as, "What are you making?" "What part are you working on right now?" and "How can I support you as a writer?" will help student writing teachers begin their conversation with a peer. These questions are also ones I want all writers to think about each day, no matter whether they are the writing teacher or not. When kids ask themselves these questions before they begin writing, they are setting a goal and making a plan to achieve it. When writers make plans and actively practice, these are steps toward independence and agency.

Then, as I teach my writing minilessons unit by unit on craft moves such as ways to find topic ideas, how to structure writing, ways to elaborate, and how to punctuate and spell accurately, I weave in conferring points that are more specific and ask students to think about one aspect of their writing. The student writing teacher can ask these questions of others, but more importantly, all writers can ask these questions of themselves. I create the anchor chart in Table 6.1 and teach students to switch the pronoun from *you* or *we* to *I* or *me* depending on who they are speaking with.

Table 6.1 An anchor chart of possible coaching moves for student writing teachers as they work with their peers and reflect on their own writing.

WAYS TO COACH OURSELVES AND OTHERS	
Setting Goals	• What are you working on as a writer? • What is your next step?
Choosing a Topic	• Look at your identity frame. What topic ideas could you write about? • Look at books in the classroom library. What topic ideas do these books make you think about?
Structuring Your Writing	• Reread your lead. Read the lead in a mentor text. What could you try as a writer? • Reread your ending. Read the ending in a mentor text. What could you try as a writer?
Elaboration– Saying More	• Reread your story and find places where you can make your character talk and move. What should the character say and do? • Find the most important part of your writing. How can you help the reader to picture your writing in their minds?
Conventions– Can Your Readers Read Your Writing?	• Reread your writing and pay attention to the punctuation. Where do you need to add or change the punctuation? • Reread your writing and pay attention to capital letters. Do you have capital letters at the beginning of each sentence, in the title, and on all names? • Reread your writing and point to each word. Stop at each tricky word and look at each part of the word. Use your mini sound book and your word wall to fix your spelling.

I intentionally place spelling and conventions in the last row because I want students to think about the meaning of what they are writing first. Conventions are important, but I don't want them to be the only way students talk about writing. I know how tempting it is for kids to see punctuation and spelling mistakes and point them out. So first I want them to focus on topic development, structure, and elaboration.

Student Writing Teachers Versus Writing Partners

The student writing teacher doesn't replace our work with writing partners. Kids still meet with writing partners during the group share time and over the course of a unit of study. Your writing partner is someone who knows your writing intimately and sees your growth. Student writing teachers are there to give in-the-moment writing guidance, and also to learn from a variety of writers in the classroom because as they move from student to student they see new writing possibilities. The most important aspect of the student writing teacher is that this role gives each student a moment to lead, a moment to be the teacher—a literacy leadership moment.

When we enable students to take on the role of the teacher, it helps solidify what they know. It also helps them step back from their own writing process and take pride in their skills as writers. I am hopeful that the student writing teacher will help kids celebrate the accomplishments of others, as well as reflect on their own growth as writers—even if all students are not as skilled at conferring as Sam. If a child simply listens and sees what other students write, it could spark a new idea and motivate a child to write and practice more.

✔ Creating More Formal Literacy Leadership Moments: Teaching Seminars

To create even more opportunities for literacy leadership moments and help children experience the power of teaching in the classroom, I build in occasions to teach others more formally a few times a year. Generally, I incorporate a "formal" teaching opportunity into one reading, writing, and math unit over the course of the year. This way, students can take the lead in different domains.

During one of our late fall literacy units, readers learn strategies to solve unfamiliar words and how to create mind movies to deepen their understanding of texts. This is a perfect unit to launch reading seminars, a more formal teaching experience for students. Reading seminars is just a fancy way of saying student-led small groups. I call them seminars because the kids who are attending sign up for the lesson that interests them the most.

To launch the idea of leading reading seminars with my class, I pose this question, "Several of you have asked if you can teach the class. Since so many kids want to show what they have learned, would you be interested in leading reading seminars?" The word *seminar* piques their curiosity. I continue, "Reading seminars are when you teach others what you have learned and you lead a small-group lesson for other students. I could show you how to plan a lesson and then we could teach some first graders. What do you think?"

Cheers erupt throughout the room!

Now that students are taken with the idea, I have to figure out how to make this happen. To help kids plan their lessons, I first show them a lesson from a previous year's student.

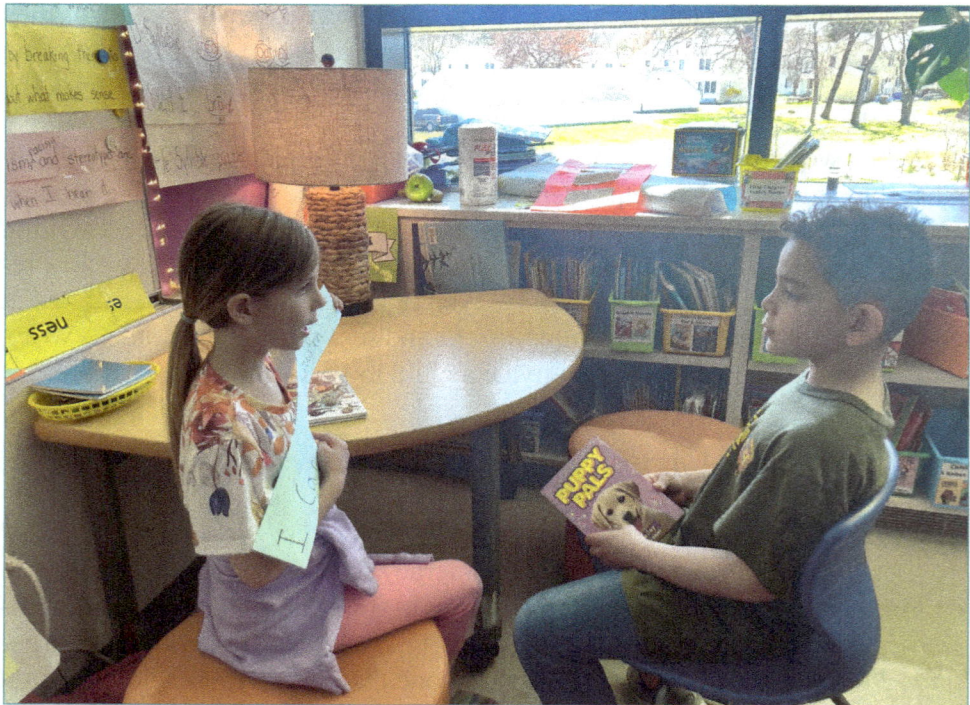

Figure 6.2
A student teaches a peer in a reading seminar.

Then I break the teaching into steps that are manageable for the kids to complete over the next several days.

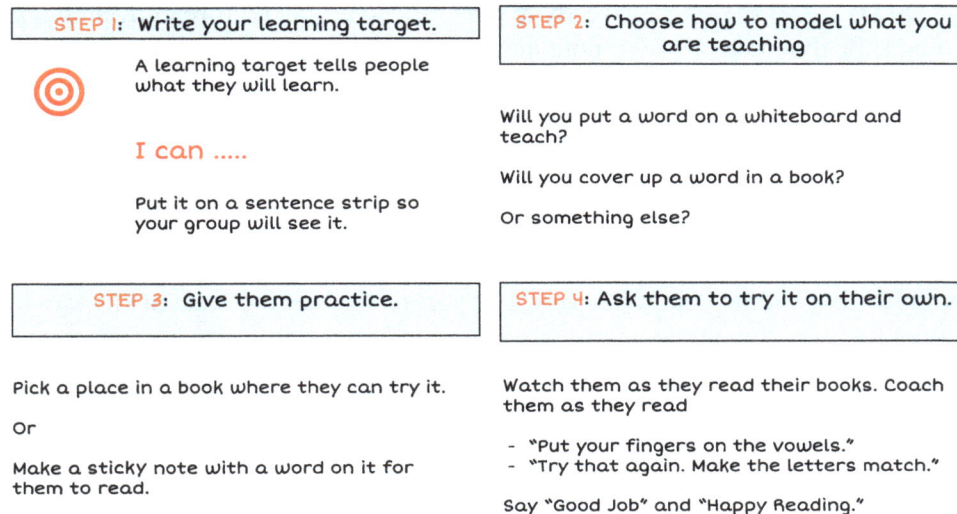

STEP 1: Write your learning target.	STEP 2: Choose how to model what you are teaching
A learning target tells people what they will learn. **I can .....** Put it on a sentence strip so your group will see it.	Will you put a word on a whiteboard and teach? Will you cover up a word in a book? Or something else?
STEP 3: Give them practice.	STEP 4: Ask them to try it on their own.
Pick a place in a book where they can try it. Or Make a sticky note with a word on it for them to read.	Watch them as they read their books. Coach them as they read - "Put your fingers on the vowels." - "Try that again. Make the letters match." Say "Good Job" and "Happy Reading."

Figure 6.3
A series of steps to support students as they plan their reading seminars for younger students.

On Day One, we write our learning targets. Students think about what they have practiced themselves in the unit and use the language from the anchor charts in our classroom to craft a learning target. Figure 6.4 shows an example from one student.

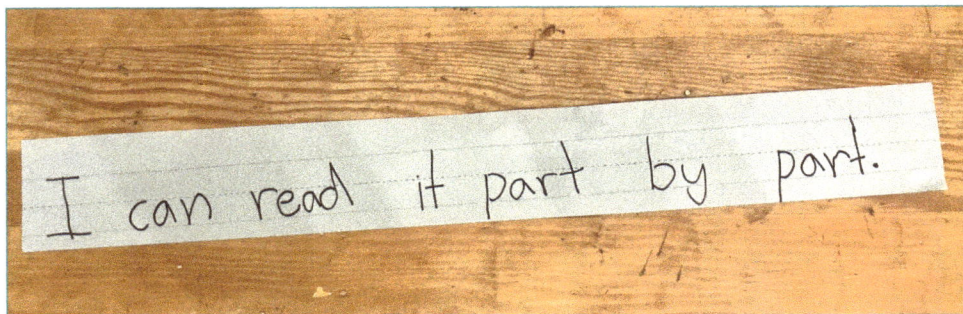

Figure 6.4
A student writes a learning target in preparation for teaching a reading seminar to younger students.

After the students write learning targets, they go back to reading their books and think about when they use the strategies. This small step keeps their lesson planning manageable and does not distract them from reading their books.

On Day Two students are ready to plan how to model their reading strategy. To do this, they take a sticky note and place it on parts of a text that they will use to demonstrate the reading strategy. If a student is teaching how to decode tricky words, the student will choose words in a book that help them show how to break a word apart. If a student is teaching how to read punctuation, they might choose a page in a book with dialogue so they can explain how a reader knows who is speaking. When a student wants to teach how to create mind movies as you read, they look for a page with lots of action so the reader can picture what the character does. The part of the text the student chooses to model their reading strategy isn't always a perfect match. They are only seven and eight years old, after all. However, the process of thinking about how to teach something helps students reflect on when and why readers use specific strategies, and that thinking process is more important than the end result.

At the end of reading workshop, we gather on the rug, and I introduce step three [Figure 6.3]—give your learners practice. Right at the rug, students place another sticky note in their book where their participants could give the strategy a try.

Now it is time for the kids to practice their lessons. To provide scaffolding to those who aren't sure how to begin their lesson, I give students some sentence starters they can use. Sentence starters such as those in Figure 6.5 help kids get their teaching point across to others.

Today I want to teach you how to _____

_____ is important because _____

Watch me. (You show how to do it)

Let's try it together. (You ask them to do it)

Now you read your book and try _____

Thank you and Happy Reading!

Figure 6.5
Sentence starters can be helpful as students plan their lessons.

After a bit of practice, it is time to begin teaching. Each of my students sets up a small-group teaching station in different areas of the room, and, as the younger students enter, they begin their lessons. Then, once the lesson is finished, my students partner read a book with the younger students in their group, coaching them as they read.

During the reading seminars, I watch Maya closely. She chose to teach others about how to look closely at the vowels in a word to help you decide which sound the vowel will make. She begins, "Readers, when you get to a tricky word, put your finger on the vowels in the word. Are there consonants after the vowel or is there a vowel team? Then she held up her whiteboard with the words *bath* and *team*. How many vowels are in this word? Right, there is only one and the th is after the vowel. This means the vowel will probably say, 'aaah.'" The lesson goes on.

Maya's voice is confident. Her language is clear, and she demonstrates the phonics skills correctly. Then, as the younger children begin to read their own books, Maya coaches them. "Yes, that is right. Look at the vowel. Nice solving that tricky word." She taught a skill that took her many quick and frequent moments to learn herself—a moment of leadership.

As I watch the kids teach, I smile. Children who were nervous sit up a bit taller, and their voices sound bolder. There are lots of smiles from our younger learners too. I loved seeing the way they look admiringly into the eyes of my students who are only one year older than them. I hope this moment helps children realize all they have to share.

One thing I try to remember when planning these teaching opportunities is that our learners who have to work hard to understand a concept are often the best teachers. Honoring their hard work by noticing their expertise and encouraging them to share it with others is a way to solidify their own understanding and help them celebrate their accomplishments. These opportunities can be literacy leadership moments for the entire class.

7

Quick and Frequent Moves to Connect with Families

It's 7:00 p.m. on a Thursday evening in September, and all of the faculty are at school. Yes—it's curriculum night, and as a team, we have spent hours preparing. While we've briefly met most of our families when they came the day before school to visit the classroom for the first time, tonight is the time set aside to give the grown-ups at home an overview of what second graders learn and explain a few highlights of the year.

When I hear footsteps entering the second-grade wing of the school, I go to the classroom door to greet people. I smile and wave as people walk right past my room and down the hallway to other spaces. Now it is 7:10 p.m. and I am alone in my classroom. After ten minutes of fidgeting with the materials I prepared, I walk and peek into nearby classrooms. Some of them are filled with many adults while others have just a few visitors. When I return to my room, it is still empty.

Now I don't know what to do. I have to stay in my room in case someone shows up, but I'm having a hard time just sitting there staring at the walls. So I begin to plan some upcoming lessons even though I know this is the wrong time to start a project—I really can't concentrate.

After a few more minutes, Maya's parent enters my room and now, with just the two of us in the classroom, it is awkward for both of us. We talk about how I see Maya look out for her younger sister even while she is at school. I show her a recent running record of Maya reading *Hello, Crabby*. We look at a phonics assessment, and I give her some word cards with digraphs and a game to play at home. Then we sit together and look through Maya's writing folder and marvel at the writing pieces her daughter has already created.

After Maya's mom leaves, I turn out the classroom lights and leave. I am deflated. While talking with Maya's mom was lovely, this initial attempt to meet with all my students' families wasn't successful. I know I need to find a different way.

After feeling a bit sorry for myself, I begin researching ways to build strong teacher–parent communication. The articles and papers I read help me generate this to-do list:

- Step 1: Figure out quick and frequent ways to communicate with each family.
- Step 2: Find and share quick and frequent ideas to support their child's practice time at home.
- Step 3: Build quick and frequent opportunities for families and caregivers to be a part of the classroom.

✔ Step 1: Quick and Frequent Ways to Communicate with Each Family

My first thought after the unsuccessful curriculum night was, "Perhaps families would rather communicate with me online. After all, Covid changed the way so many of us communicate. Maybe digital communication is preferable." So I create a Google Form that asks families three questions:

1. What communication method works best for you?
2. What questions do you have about second grade?
3. Is there anything you would like me to know about your child?

Unfortunately, this attempt at communication didn't go much better. Six families responded. Now, don't get me wrong, six is better than nothing, but what about the other two-thirds of the class? I still needed a different entry point.

Quick and Frequent Communication: Sending Photos

I wondered what would happen if I captured photos of each individual child in the classroom and sent those home with a quick but personal note. Would folks reply? I was taking photos of the kids anyway so it would be easy to email a photo. Over the next week, I snapped photos with my phone and sent this message:

> Hi _____ *[name of child's caregiver],*
>
> _____ *[child's name] worked hard on* _____
> *[learning goal] today.*
>
> *Enjoy!*
>
> *Tammy (aka—Mrs. Mulligan)*

Now I started to get responses. Many people wrote back thanking me and sometimes they also shared how their child was feeling at school. As quickly as I could, I emailed them back with one request. "I'm so glad you liked the photo. I'll send more via a platform called Seesaw. Seesaw is a secure website so I'll be able to share more class photos because the children's privacy will be protected. Here is the link. Would you mind signing up?"

This strategy worked for 90 percent of the households. Emailing a few photos created a back-and-forth communication. First off, families knew how to reach me through email, and I knew they received the information I sent. In addition, once I connected with the grown-ups at home on a personal level, they followed up and clicked on the link to sign up for Seesaw. This was perfect as now I had two ways to communicate with most people.

Sending an email with a photo also helped me know which households didn't receive this communication, or at least hadn't responded. It was just a few, so I called them during the school day to share something positive—a moment their child showed kindness, a time their child took the lead, or a moment their child persevered through something difficult.

I also explained that I had a photo from school to share and asked them what the best way to send it was. Most families hadn't received the photo I had sent previously and gave me an alternate email or their cell phone number. Once again, I sent the photo with a message about signing up for Seesaw. After just a week of these small communications, I had reached every household, and they were all connected through Seesaw. Although my attempts at communication weren't successful at first, the rough start taught me some things—start with photos, share joys from the classroom, and build from there.

Quick and Frequent Communication: Sharing Videos of Classroom Life

Now that I had the entire class linked through Seesaw, I used this communication tool to help families get a peek into life in the classroom. Once a week in the fall, I sent home a twenty- to thirty-second video of the students working in each subject area.

To begin, I explained to the students that one part of my job as their teacher was to be a team with their grown-ups at home. Being a team meant that I needed to share what we do at school, and sending short videos is one way I can do that. I explained to the students that these videos could also be helpful to them too. They could watch them with a grown-up and explain what they are learning at school and tell them more about our classroom. This talk about the purpose of the videos helped the students understand that they should ignore the camera and continue working. It wasn't a time to wave or smile for the camera, but I promised there would be other times for that. I also reassured students that I would show them the videos before I sent them home. This way they could also see how hard we are all working individually and as a community at school.

Creating these videos was simple. When the room was settled and students were working, I told the students I would be videoing for one minute and they should continue working. Then I grabbed the classroom iPad and took a twenty- to thirty-second video. Sometimes, I narrated as the video was being recorded and said aloud what the students were doing. "Hi, everyone. The kids are hard at work during writing workshop. They are writing true stories and are working on telling the story with small actions and dialogue." Then, I put the iPad away and conferred with students.

At the end of the day, I showed the video to the students so they could discuss all of the positive work habits they noticed. Then, when the kids left for the day, I uploaded the video to Seesaw and sent it to families with a quick note.

> *Hello Second-Grade Families,*
>
> *Look at all the writers hard at work creating true stories about their lives.*
>
> *Enjoy,*
>
> *Tammy (aka—Mrs. Mulligan)*

Throughout the first months of school, I sent videos that showed snippets of hands-down conversations so everyone at home could see the kinds of discussions we have about texts. I also sent videos of how our classroom community works together. Families saw videos of the class singing during morning meeting and how kids read together during partner reading. Then, later in the year, when we performed Reader's Theater plays, I sent videos of those home too.

I think these videos helped me make connections and build trust with folks at home. These peeks into the school day make classroom life a bit more accessible to families, no matter whether they pick up their child in person each day or they physically visit the classroom. My goal is for everyone to have information about what happens during the school day.

These first connections also make difficult conversations a bit easier. Since my students' families have an image of what happens at school and know a little bit about how the classroom works, they feel more trust that the classroom environment is safe and supportive of their child. Then, when problems arise, we can work together to problem-solve to support their child. Of course, this is not true in every situation, but I believe these videos help bring us all a little closer.

✔ Step 2: Quick and Frequent Ideas to Support Families with Home Practice

A few months into the school year, once I have a more consistent audience on Seesaw, I also create two- to three-minute videos for families to learn more about the curriculum. About twice a month, I put a reminder in my plan book to create a video about one concept about which the students were learning. Here are some of the video topics that relate to literacy and some snippets of what I have said on these topics:

- **Making reading at home as joyful as possible**

  Our goal together is to help your child develop as a reader—someone who can read and someone who wants to read. To do this, I want to help make reading at home as joyful as possible. For some kids it helps to have someone to read to—a stuffed animal, a pet, or anyone at home, or even someone they can FaceTime. For other kids, where they read matters—a comfy spot with a pillow, or somewhere with a yummy snack or a tasty drink. Some children do best when they read in short bursts—reading in the car, waiting in a line, reading a little bit in the afternoon and more before bed. Others read a lot in one sitting. All kinds of reading will make a difference, so it is essential that they read. However, how they do that is up to you. Please email me if you want to chat. I am happy to problem-solve together if that is helpful. As with all of these videos, these are just suggestions. Use what is helpful and ignore the rest.

- **Supporting readers as they solve tricky words**

    At school, the children are learning phonetic patterns so they can look closely at the letters to decode a word, and then make sure what they said matches the letters and makes sense. Today I sent home a bookmark with some steps to solve a word. [I read the steps on the bookmark.] Let me show you what this sounds like with a word. [I model these steps on video.]

    Sometimes, when kids are home, this process doesn't go as well as it does at school. If solving a word becomes problematic in any way (the book is too difficult, your child becomes emotional), please tell the child the word. Making reading joyful at home so it becomes a regular habit is the priority. I teach phonics every day and your child's skills will grow. If you would like to chat, please email me. I am happy to listen and problem-solve together.

- **Supporting readers when a text is difficult**

    To support fluent reading and keep reading at home joyful, I help children choose books that they can read with about 96–98 percent accuracy, but sometimes the book they bring home isn't a helpful choice. Please do not feel that your child needs to read the book they brought home. Instead, you could read it aloud, you could take turns reading paragraphs or pages, or you could abandon the book completely. There is nothing magical about the book they bring from school. Reading texts that you have at home is a great option too. As always, please make a decision that is best for your life at home, and let me know so I can work with your child to choose something else.

- **Library books versus take-home books**

    This week your child went to the library for the first time this school year. Each week your child will bring home two library books in addition to the take-home book they take from the classroom. During library time, kids get to choose anything from the library, no matter how difficult, and that is a good thing. If they want to bring home that Star Wars book six weeks in a row, they can. Your child also chose the take-home book, but the selection is much narrower. I have helped your child to find a book they can read accurately.

Sometimes, all these books are great for reading independently and sometimes they are not. Please use your judgment about which books to read aloud to your child, which books your child will just look through, and which texts your child will read independently. When kids try to read texts that are very difficult, they can become deflated. Let me know how I can support your kiddos in deciding how to read each book.

- **Reading over breaks**

I've been talking to the kids about how readers make plans when our schedules change and we have more time. We've talked about how readers sometimes listen to audiobooks during long car rides, they read when they wake up, or they might keep a book with them for when they have some extra free time. Since our winter break is coming, the kids made a plan for what they want to read, and when they want to read over break. [I show the plan.] Please know that each child selected several books to take with them. It doesn't matter whether they read these texts or others. What matters is that they find time to read. Their skills are so new and they have made such growth that we want them to continue on this path, and reading over break will help. As always, please email me if you want to chat and problem-solve together.

- **Expanding reading choices—Video 1**

A few of you have reached out because your child insists on reading the same book again and again or wants to read every book in a particular series. In general, I want you to know that these are normal parts of reading development. Reading the same book again and again, or reading the same series, can promote fluency. Through this process, children learn to read with expression, and they also increase the words they read automatically. Now, sometimes kids do need to move on because they have memorized the entire text and they are no longer actually reading the text. Please reach out if you feel your child is not reading an appropriate text choice. I am happy to think this through together.

- **Expanding reading choices—Video II**

Up until this point, the children have brought home books to read, but reading is so much more than just reading books. Please encourage your child to read directions, recipes, shopping lists, road signs, maps, or any other environmental print. There are also many online resources. Here are a few online options that may also be great choices for reading at home. [Then I share my screen and show websites such as Read-Along Toon Books, Wonderopolis, and Dogonews.] Readers need choices so feel free to expand what your child reads beyond the books that come home each day.

The list of possible video topics is endless. I find these topics by thinking about my teaching points at school, the kids' reflections about how reading at home is going and what the people at home share with me. In all of these messages, my main themes are that kids need to practice, and that practice can be joyful. I also encourage families to reach out in any moment. Helping readers grow and develop readerly identities is a process that takes consistency and collaboration. These videos are one quick and frequent way I communicate in an effort to connect with folks at home.

To keep the video process simple, I have a few self-imposed rules:

- Making the video needs to take a lot less time than writing the same information in an email.
- Ninety-five percent of the videos I create are done in one take.
- I will not refresh my makeup before I tape.
- Videos will be no longer than three minutes.

To create a video, I jot down on a scrap piece of paper what I want to teach families and caregivers. For example, if I am creating a video about ways to solve tricky words, my notes would say—put your fingers on the vowels, read each part, and put the parts together. Then I take a small whiteboard and write down two words to model this concept for everyone at home.

After that, I sit in front of my laptop right in the classroom. This way the empty classroom is my backdrop, and viewers can get a glimpse of our classroom space. I record the video right in Seesaw, watch it once to make sure it recorded, write a short note, and press Send. Here is an example of what a typical note from me looks like:

Hi Second-Grade Families,

Here are some photos of the kids reading at school. Tonight your child will bring home a book to read. Here is a one-minute video about homework in second grade and some tips for what to do when your child encounters an unfamiliar word when reading.

Thank you,

Tammy (aka—Mrs. Mulligan)

In the Seesaw app, I can see how many people viewed a video so I have a sense of how many households I reach. I also know the videos are working because kids come into school and say, "I watched your video last night." This comment is helpful on two fronts: (1) I know that a family saw the video, and (2) I am reminded that kids are watching these videos and I want to keep that in mind when I create them.

Of course, these videos about ways to help at home don't replace sending home individual photos, calling to problem-solve a situation, or sharing individual accomplishments. What viewers say about the Seesaw communication is that it helps them know what is going on in the classroom, and they appreciate the quick update. One mom shared, "Thanks for the videos. They are quick and to the point. It is just what I need to know to be able to help at home."

The videos I create reduce the amount of written communication I send, so they save my time as well. Based on the feedback I receive, they work for many adults at home too—a classic win-win in communication.

Literacy Leadership Moments: Let the Kids Create Videos

Another way families know how to help at home is through videos I periodically have kids create about their accomplishments. When a child finishes reading a text and is proud, or when they try a new craft move in writing, or when they solve a tricky math problem, I will ask them if they want to show their work on Seesaw and explain what they did.

To support children to notice and name their literacy leadership moments, I create a list with the class about possible topics to share with the grown-ups at home. The lists below are certainly not exhaustive, but we create these ideas unit by unit over the course of the year. Generally, children choose a topic that is important to them—one they have practiced. Sometimes their ideas about what to video come from my small-group lessons and individual conferences with them. But other times they are entirely child generated. These informal videos are all about celebrating the practice students are working on and what they have achieved. Here are just some of the topics about which children have created videos. You can see that many of these topics align with the grade-level state standards.

Video topics about growth as readers:

- Solving a tricky word
- Focusing when I read to build my stamina
- Figuring out what a word means by thinking about the meaning of the text
- Visualizing a scene while reading
- Determining how a character feels and why they feel that way
- Thinking about a theme of a text
- Retelling the main events in a fictional text
- Retelling an informational text by teaching about the subtopics and details
- Explaining the setting of a text and how that setting impacts the problem
- Describing the overall problem the characters face
- Describing how the character solves a problem
- Giving a book talk about why others should read this text
- Reading a part of text fluently
- Explaining how to read the punctuation in a text
- Celebrating a text I finished reading

Video topics about growth as a word solver and speller:

- Using letter sounds to read a word
- Practicing letter sounds to become automatic
- Writing multisyllabic words
- Writing words with silent e
- Writing words with blends and/or digraphs
- Ways to use phonics sound cards to help you write a word
- Practicing reading and/or spelling high-frequency words

Video topics about growth as writers:

- Finding a topic idea
- Planning my writing once I have an idea
- Setting goals and improving my writing stamina
- Organizing my writing in a way that makes sense for the genre

- Ways to say more about a topic or an idea
- Adding thoughts, action, and dialogue to my writing
- Embedding the setting throughout my story
- Revising my writing
- Editing my writing for spelling
- Editing my writing for capital letters
- Punctuating my writing
- Celebrating a piece of writing I finished

To help kids create videos that are meaningful, I give them possible steps to follow and some sentence starter options to scaffold their talk. Before video-taping, kids think about what they want to say. Since I want kids to make these videos frequently (approximately one per month), I need to make this work efficient and productive. So instead of having kids write out exactly what they are going to say, I have students glue the sentence frames below into the back of their community notebook. Then, when they are almost ready to record, I ask them to open to this page of their notebook and orally rehearse what they want to say. In general, kids do not write their words down as I want them to be able to speak freely on the videos, but I do have them practice a bit with these sentence starters in mind. They know that they don't have to use them and should use what helps them create a video that is clear to the listener. This way the videos are authentic and there are some supports to help kids create videos that are quick and focused.

"I learned how to _____."

"First I _____. Then I _____."

"I'm really (proud, excited, _____) because _____."

[Show or read your work.]

One afternoon, after practicing reading and writing silent e words for a few weeks, I asked Sam to make a video about reading and writing silent e words. I thought Sam would just grab his phonics sound book and write one word on a whiteboard and make the video. But Sam surprised me and took it much further than that. He put together a whole lesson. First Sam showed how to practice the two sounds a vowel makes. Then he explained how the words *cap* and *cape* are the same and different. He finished off by reading an entire chapter. As he read words with silent e, he explained how to solve them. This video was a bit long, but I didn't care. Sam was so proud of what he had learned and that was all that mattered.

When students create these videos, I often send a note home at the beginning of the week to everyone so that they can be on the lookout for a notification from Seesaw. I tell people to let me know if they don't see a video. I try to keep track, but every once in a while, someone's video is sitting on their iPad in draft form because the student forgot to press Submit. This is why I give families a timeframe for when they should see it. Then, if they don't, they let me know and I can fix the problems. Here is a type of quick note I send home on Seesaw.

> *Hello,*
>
> *Please be on the lookout for a Seesaw video from your child. As they finish their first small moment story, they will share it with you on Seesaw and tell you what they tried as writers. If you don't see it by Friday, please let me know.*
>
> *Thank you,*
>
> *Tammy (aka—Mrs. Mulligan)*

One day, after I introduced creating videos to highlight our learning, Maya turned to me. "Mrs. Mulligan, you know how I am reading new books each week?"

"Yes," I answered.

"What if, after I practiced a book for a few times, I made a video for my little sister? We could watch them at home, and I could teach her how to read." So that is what we did. Every few weeks, Maya read her book aloud into Seesaw. She practiced her fluency by rereading and her videos enabled her to help a younger sibling—another literacy leadership moment for Maya.

Each year I incorporate more and more student reflection into my practice. Student-created videos are a quick and frequent way to communicate with families with little effort on my part. The grown-ups at home get to see what their child creates, and students get a chance to stop, notice, and self-reflect on their progress. As the end of the year approaches, students love to spend time watching videos they made in the fall and marvel at all they have learned. I love it too—it gives me a chance to step back from the busyness of classroom life and see how much students have learned.

✔ Step 3: Quick and Frequent Ways for Families and Caregivers to Be Part of the Classroom

When I first thought about inviting folks from home into the classroom, I was hesitant. Being a working mom myself, I understand that not everyone can make time during the school day to come to school and I don't want to set up an equity issue that advantages some children over others. So instead, I plan multiple opportunities for families to come into the room that include in-person one-time events and virtual live events.

Families Sharing Expertise in Fifteen-Minute Spurts

This project started with a large world map and a United States map mounted on the classroom wall. To begin, each child chose a place on the map that was important to them. Since almost all of the children have lived in multiple places (all of the families in my classroom are military families), they have many options. Some children place their pin where they were born, some choose where they are moving next, others pick the place where their parents grew up or a spot where a family member is currently stationed. And, of course, some pick a place simply because they love it or are interested in it.

After choosing places on the maps, students spend time in small groups telling stories about their chosen place and why it is meaningful to them. Some children choose to add photos and/or drawings of this place to their identity frames (see Chapter 5) to honor their memories and places they have lived, and others simply explain aloud to their small group why they chose their place. Either is fine as this is a starting place for learning about one another and the places that matter to us. To include the grown-ups at home in this work, I sent home a photo of our maps with this note.

> *Hi Families,*
>
> *We need your help. Second graders learn about world geography and how it impacts people. Since many of you have lived in places all over the United States and the world, I am hoping you can help. Would you be able to come into the classroom (live or virtually) for fifteen minutes and tell us about a place you know? The kids would love to learn about any of the fifty states or any other place in the world. All you will need are four or five images (photos you took or ones from the internet) to share.*

Please email back if you can help and I will send you more details.

Thanks,

Tammy (aka—Mrs. Mulligan)

After sending this note to families I received several responses and followed up with some phone calls. Some family members came into the classroom in person to tell their experiences in a place outside of Massachusetts (the state where we live) and others joined the class virtually. From New York, Florida, and Ohio to Korea, China, and Puerto Rico, families used maps and pictures to tell a bit about the geography of a place and how this place impacted their lives.

On the mornings of these visits, the students generated a list of possible questions to ask the presenter. I recorded these questions on chart paper so that they could be seen when our guest arrived. After the person spoke for five or ten minutes, students asked questions from this list or questions that they thought of in the moment based on what they learned in the short presentation. Having some of the questions listed ahead of time helped the visitor see information that interested the kids and also made the presentation a bit more interactive.

No matter whether a family member presented virtually or in person, I asked families to send me the photos they wanted to share. Most sent the photos in PowerPoint or Google Slides, but one or two just sent the images via email and I quickly put them into a slide deck. Having the photos ahead of time gave me a glimpse of what the family member would be sharing. Then I could have the photos on my computer ready for the presentation so all they had to do was use the classroom remote control to advance the slides. This way we avoided any connectivity issues and lag time. The person was able to start their presentation as soon as they entered the room, and they headed out of the class after fifteen or twenty minutes. This was just the right amount of time for students' attention spans.

When a family member presented virtually, I made some slight changes. First, the family member introduced themselves to the kids and I pointed my camera at the kids so they could see their audience and say hello to their child. Then the virtual visitor showed their slides and spoke while the student listened for five to ten minutes. After that, they stopped sharing their screen and came back in front of the camera to answer the kids' questions.

Having these two options made it easier for more people to be a part of the classroom during their workday, or even from a faraway place. And while I know the population I teach is unique in that they have lived in many places, I also know that every community is unique in some way. All families have special places worthy of being shared with their child's classroom community.

✔ Literacy Leadership Moment: Student-Led Parent–Teacher Conferences

A couple of years ago my fall parent–teacher conferences were a mixed success. Many families signed up for an in-person or virtual conference, but some did not. When I followed up with reminder emails, I was only partially successful. Some people still chose not to attend. Then, when conference day arrived, several families who scheduled a conference did not show up for their designated time. This traditional scheduled conference format with a virtual option just wasn't working for all families.

A month before spring conferences my colleague, Andrea Defina, shared a brilliant idea: student-led parent–teacher conferences. Now, instead of families meeting with me alone, the children would lead and share their learning with their families. I sent home this note with a video explaining this idea:

Dear Families,

I am excited to announce that students will lead the spring parent–teacher conferences! Student-led conference days will be March 29th and April 5th from 1:30–4:00 pm. Spring conferences will focus on the following:

1. Student social-emotional growth, engagement, and sense of belonging.

2. Student learning and academic development.

3. How teachers and families can support students during the remainder of the school year.

Each student-led conference will be twenty minutes, but you will notice that the time slots are set in fifteen-minute increments. There will be a five-minute overlap between families. The extra allotted time allows for students to begin the conference independently before I join in.

If you would like an additional private one-on-one conference (without your child), you can sign up for one of the time slots I set aside on Wednesday, April 12th. Please reach out if you have any questions or concerns. See you soon! Here is the link where you can sign up.

Thanks,

Tammy (aka—Mrs. Mulligan)

This time, instead of sending reminders, families signed up immediately and kids came into school clamoring about what they would share during their conference.

To help kids get ready for their conference, my colleague and I used a checklist that asked each child to self-reflect on their work habits [Figure 7.1]. The checklist asked children to rate their work habits using a scale of always, often, sometimes, and never.

I read the choices aloud and then the kids worked independently to reflect on their work habits. Over the next few days, I met with each student individually and listened as they shared their reflections with me. Then I placed a tiny heart in each of the columns to show the student (and their family) where I thought the student was. In most cases, students were more critical of themselves than I was, and I wanted the kids and their families to see how hard their students were working and learning.

Figure 7.1
A student records her reflections about her work habits and preferences at school.

The week before conferences began, students spent time collecting arti-facts of their learning. They began by reflecting on their growth as readers. With colorful sticky notes in hand, they selected a page from a book to read aloud to their family to highlight their word-solving skills or their fluent read-ing. Once they found the page, students wrote a quick note on the sticky note explaining what they wanted to share.

Students also chose a place in their book where they had done some im-portant thinking. After reviewing some of the stop-and-jots in their books, they decided which of their notes demonstrated their thinking about the problem in the story, the character's feelings, or a theme of the text.

Next, we moved on to writing and students selected pieces of writing to show their families. Again, they repeated this same process—they reread their work and placed sticky notes on one or two spots in their writing where they had tried a specific writer's craft move.

Students placed all of their work for their conference in a folder and now it was time to practice. They lined up outside the classroom and pretended they were arriving with their family. Then they grabbed their conference folder with all of their work, practiced showing their family around the classroom, and then, with a partner, had a mock parent conference in which they ex-plained what they had learned and why it was important to them. I also joined each of these sessions, so students would understand that I would also attend the conference and add onto what they were sharing.

After a few days of reflection and practice, we were as prepared as we could be, and it was time to begin. When I opened Google Calendar to see the number of appointments I had for the first day of conferences, my stomach clenched. I had ten conferences back to back. Would families arrive on time? Would I be able to attend every conference? Would the kids feel successful? Would the conferences be valuable to both kids and families? I have to admit, I was worried. I knew how tired I was when I had seven or eight conferences in a day—ten felt overwhelming.

But I needn't have worried; this conference day took my breath away. I watched Jory share how she learned to solve a hard word by putting her fin-gers on the vowels and breaking the words. I watched Maya share her excite-ment about reading the first four books in the *Owl Diaries* series. I watched Sam read aloud a favorite page from *King and Kayla*. These kids and all their classmates shared their learning journeys with the people in their lives. They read aloud and explained reading strategies they learned, they told stories about how they decided on their writing topics, and also shared moments when learning was hard and what they had done to persevere.

Instead of delivering information to families, I listened, I laughed alongside students, and I shared bits of information that built off of what students said. As students showed families around the room, I also got to see what students cared about and what they valued in our classroom. As families exited the room, many commented on how much they loved this conference format and how proud they were of what their child shared. I have to say that I left that evening feeling exhilarated rather than exhausted. At the end of the spring conferences, all families had attended, and the kids had done a significant amount of self-reflection.

For me, these parent–teacher conferences were a reminder that low-stakes ways of inviting folks into school can make a difference. After one student-led conference, a family member pulled me aside and thanked me. He had never entered a school since he himself left high school, and his plan was to never enter one again. He just said, "School is really different now, and I'm glad my daughter is happy here." He helped me remember that we never know someone else's story, and it is part of my job to make school a comfortable and safe place for the adults that care for the students we teach.

✔ A Path Forward

Planning quick and frequent instruction has become my path forward—from the overwhelmed and frustrated to joyful and impactful teaching. I started this process by focusing on each student's next steps in reading. But this focus for quick and frequent practice morphed into something much larger. It became a way for students to think about themselves and their goals and plan their own next steps. Throughout the year, students practiced with me several times a day, every day. But, in addition, students designed their own practice in all areas of learning. The notion of planning quick and frequent practice when you want to learn something new, get better at something, or solve a problem became a mantra for how to reach our goals. I think Sam said it best, when reflecting at the end of the year, that he had learned to "never give up." For Sam, and many other students, they needed opportunities to see the power of quick and frequent practice, to see how many small moments, many small actions add up to powerful learning.

Through my work in the classroom, I now realize that quick and frequent practice isn't *just* about teaching skills in short bursts. There are four main facets of quick and frequent practice that must be in place for students to experience its full potential and integrate it into their lives.

Students need to:

1. **Participate in two- to five-minute quick and frequent sessions daily to acquire foundational skills.** As students participate, they see their growth and the impact of practice on their learning. They realize that working on something a little bit at a time can turn something that was difficult into something you actually enjoy.

2. **Learn about other people's stories of persistence and perseverance.** Students need to learn about people who didn't give up and have accomplished amazing things in our world. Other people's stories illustrate the quick and frequent steps, as well as the setbacks, that happen in life when we set out to accomplish a goal. Without the story of the journey, sometimes others' achievements can appear to come only from innate ability. Learners need to hear about the messiness along the way.

3. **Plan quick and frequent practice for themselves and for others.** Kids need to take on the role of teachers to learn how to explain, demonstrate, guide, and give feedback. Through this practice, students learn how to coach themselves and how to coach others. When they become teachers, they see the power of their ideas, and the skills that they do possess. Perceived deficits become strengths as the best teachers are sometimes people who struggled at first. It is through the struggle that we learn the whens, whats, hows, and whys of applying a strategy.

4. **Experience leadership moments that matter.** As teachers, we need to plan leadership moments into our curriculum so that they become an integral part of a child's learning experience. We can flip instruction on its head and enable the person who needs support to also have opportunities to be the person teaching others. When we do so, positive dispositions have the chance to flourish, and children can "write their story" as someone who helps others rather than someone who always needs the help of others.

When we plan our teaching with these four ideas in mind, we ultimately normalize the learning process for our students. Instead of students believing they should "just know" how to do something (or worse, think that they are not smart when something is difficult to learn) they understand that learning new things takes practice. Quick and frequent practice shows some of the ins and outs of having a growth mindset. Because after all, it is not just about what we say to ourselves when learning gets difficult, it is also about what we do—the actions we can take. I want kids to experience what a growth mindset looks like, sounds like, and feels like, while also keeping the learning goals manageable and achievable. Then these small successes can lead them to even bigger accomplishments and give students some tools to handle difficulties when they come their way.

Thinking of my teaching moves as quick and frequent changes my mindset too. It helps me keep things simple and focus on what I can do in a situation instead of becoming overwhelmed by all the things I can't control. For me, quick and frequent means taking one step at a time and trying something. What if I sent one photo home to each family? What if I list one or two concepts my students who read below grade level need and teach them in two-minute bursts? What if I introduce the kids to a new person every few weeks to help broaden their understanding of themselves and the people around them? My only way forward is to figure out quick and frequent ways to chip away at whatever obstacle or challenging situation comes my way.

When I let the hard parts of teaching cloud my mind, these hard parts swipe away the joys of teaching and the joy of being surrounded by children each day. When frustration comes, instead of saying to myself, "Well, that is out of my control," I try to step back and think about the quick and frequent moves I can try in the classroom that might chip away at the issue. This practice helps reduce my own anxiety and keep me focused on what is right in front of me. This way of thinking brings a piece of joy back to me and to the kids sitting in front of me.

And, no, my small moves don't always work. Sometimes students aren't interested in the practice I offer. Some small moves don't help me reach a student in the way I hoped. Sometimes, when the kids try to practice on their own, it isn't productive at first. Yet, even with all the missteps, some helpful ideas do emerge. So many of the quick and frequent moves in this book were born from moments of disappointment, fear, and frustration about all the things in teaching that are just plain hard.

So how does a year of learning end for Jory, Sam, and Maya? What happened to the red numbers on that spreadsheet at the start of the year? Well, most of them changed from red to yellow, and many from red to yellow and then to green. And, of course, like all children, Jory, Sam, and Maya changed and grew in marvelous ways that spreadsheets cannot capture.

Jory

According to the DIBELS end-of-year assessments and the Fountas & Pinnell Benchmark Assessment System, Jory made significant growth in many areas of reading and continues to need support in others. This assessment data shows that she can accurately decode single-syllable nonsense words on grade level and apply these strategies when reading connected text. She also has strong literal and inferential comprehension skills. An area of relative weakness for Jory continues to be her oral reading rate. Jory is now an accurate reader but reads slowly. Increasing her automaticity and fluent reading will be a continued goal for next year.

But there is so much more to Jory's reading life than what these isolated assessments reveal. During the last week of school, Jory asked, "Mrs. Mulligan, can you show me the books I read in the beginning of the year?" I walked with her to the book room as these books were no longer in our current classroom library. I picked up the Mary Ruth book, *Hold Still, Danny!* (Level D) and opened to a page. Then, I watched as she proudly showed this book to another teacher and explained, "This is what I used to read. Wow! I can't believe it."

This spring, Jory participated in a mystery book club group and fell in love with the genre. I love the smile on her face when she finishes a chapter and exclaims, "Mrs. Mulligan, I think I figured out the mystery." As she reads mysteries, she will continue to work to scoop up words into phrases so her reading sounds like talking, and in time she will become more fluent.

Jory's reading life is also only a small part of her. From our 180 days together, I see her as one of the kindest people I know. She will give up her spot in line, a preferred color marker, or a ball at recess to bring joy to someone else. In turn, people love being around Jory. She can be found with friends huddled around her at the rug laughing about a game they played on the playground. Her kindness and generosity are contagious.

Maya

Even though Maya joined the class in November, her assessment numbers on the spreadsheet also moved from red to yellow and even into some green areas. The DIBELS and Fountas & Pinnell Benchmark Assessment System show that Maya can accurately decode single-syllable nonsense words on grade level. When reading connected text, Maya stops independently at tricky words, problem-solves, and then rereads. She self-corrects routinely, and then rereads to make sure she comprehends the text. All of these skills have helped her to meet grade-level benchmarks.

Maya's need to slow down and problem-solve routinely causes her oral reading rate to be lower than the grade-level benchmark. Although she reads with expression and appropriate phrasing, a next step for Maya is to become more automatic when reading unfamiliar words. As this process becomes more automatic, her oral reading rate will improve.

This spring Maya found the *Critter Club* series by Callie Barkley and loves reading and talking about the friendship troubles in these books. She applies what she has learned in her own life about building relationships with peers to help her identify the character's feelings in a text and think about how the character should handle this problem. I remember her words during one of our reading conferences from the spring: "Mrs. Mulligan, Marion's [a character from *Critter Club*] problem is just a glitch. I think she should move on."

Maya is also an incredible big sister. When she notices that she has two snacks in her lunchbox, she immediately asks, "Mrs. Mulligan, can I go down and check on my sister? I think she might be missing her snack." She loves crafts and, for the end of the year, made each student in the class a friendship bracelet she created out of rubber bands.

Sam

Sam reached grade-level benchmarks according to the DIBELS and the Fountas & Pinnell Benchmark Assessment System. His ability to apply his knowledge of phonics grew tremendously over the year, and he has strong literal and inferential comprehension of the texts he reads. In the classroom, you can often find him tucked away reading the *Dog Man* series by Dav Pilkey. He has read the first seven books in the series and plans to read the rest. This year, he wrote me this note [Figure 7.2]. Don't you just love the really smart spelling mistakes

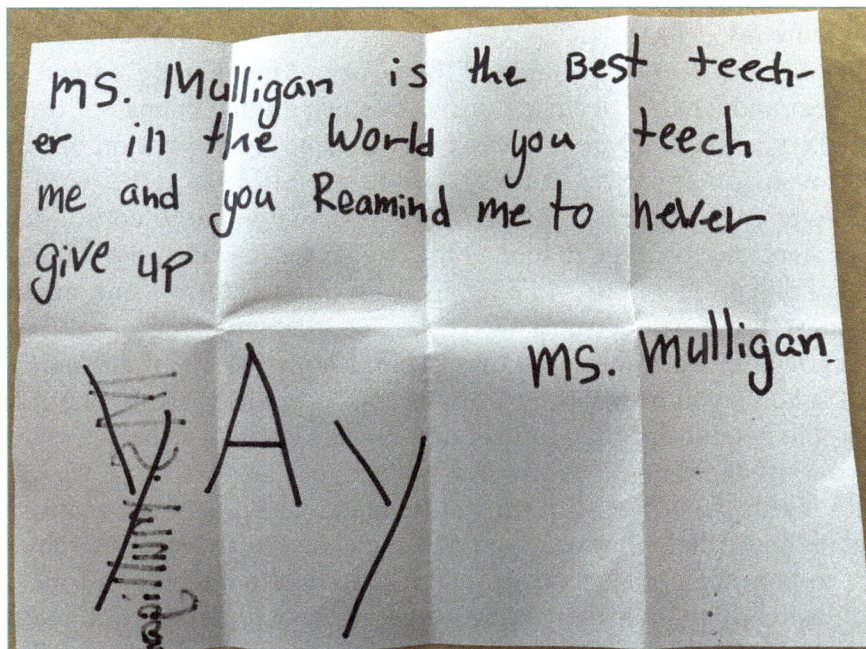

Figure 7.2
A note from Sam.

in "teech and "reamind"? He is remembering to use vowel teams and soon he will apply this new knowledge in the right places as he spells. I am so happy he made such growth, but I am even happier that he knows to never give up. That will serve him well.

Now as I sit at the end-of-year data meeting, my panic from the first data meeting has eased. I know these children well, and I also know the growth they have made and the continued practice they need. The data is not a surprise. I know my students. I know what they have learned, and I know what they have accomplished. We did it together—one small step at a time.

What I wish for all of us who have chosen to spend our days alongside kids is that we continue to persevere together. We pause, we rethink, we share, and together we find quick and frequent moves that make our classrooms impactful and joyful. So much of what happens in schools is out of our control and we have to help each other focus on the small moves that can bring our classrooms to life.

As I write the ending to this book, I can see a cardinal nest right outside my window. I watch the mother and father cardinals quickly feed their babies, fly away, fly back, sit for a short while, and repeat. It is quick and frequent, and it is impactful. The babies are getting bigger and their cries for food are getting louder each day. Their small actions are changing these baby birds right before my eyes.

This book is also an example of the power of quick and frequent work. For a year and a half, I set aside thirty- to sixty-minute chunks of time just a few days a week. At first, I was overwhelmed by the notion of writing 40,000 words on my own. But instead, I refused to look at the word count (Ruth Ayres, the editor of *Choice Literacy*, actually had to consolidate all the chapters and force me to look at the count) because it overwhelmed me. I needed this project to feel like I was just writing articles—one small step at a time.

As you head back into your classroom, I hope the mantra of quick and frequent helps you break away from feeling overwhelmed. I hope it helps you problem-solve and plan so that your biggest challenges become smaller, and your students make gains. But more importantly, I hope we can all show our kids the power of quick and frequent work, so that no matter what obstacles come their way, or what goals they want to accomplish, they have a tool to help them plan their way to success one moment at a time. This is the disposition that I really hope we can share with children. I leave you with a student's words about the power of a teacher [Figure 7.3]. What we do really does matter.

My Teacher
BY _____

You make me feel like I be long here. You are so answer you like a bight light. You are my teacher You make me fill like I can do anything. You make me feel good smart helpful. You are my teacher you can do anything. You are nice kind smart fun. thank you for being my teacher ♡

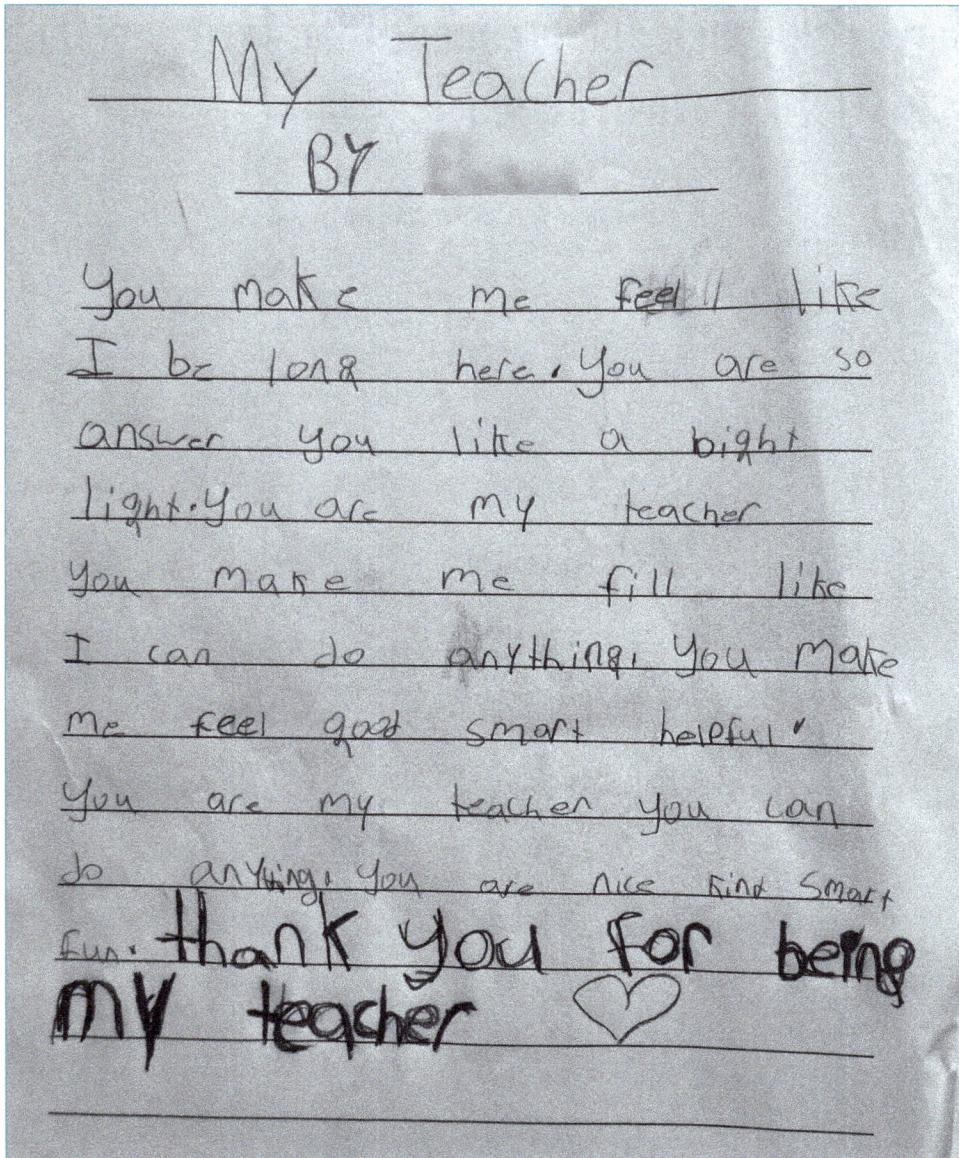

Figure 7.3
A child's poem.

Appendix A: Quick and Frequent Plan for Individualized Instruction Template

Quick and Frequent Plan for Individualized Instruction
Week of _____

NAMES	FOCUS
Monday ____Tuesday ____ Wednesday ____ Thursday ____ Friday ____	**Reading** **Writing**
Monday ____Tuesday ____ Wednesday ____ Thursday ____ Friday ____	**Reading** **Writing**
Monday ____Tuesday ____ Wednesday ____ Thursday ____ Friday ____	**Reading** **Writing**
Monday ____Tuesday ____ Wednesday ____ Thursday ____ Friday ____	**Reading** **Writing**
Monday ____Tuesday ____ Wednesday ____ Thursday ____ Friday ____	**Reading** **Writing**

Appendix B: Quick and Frequent Plan for Small-Group Instruction Template

Quick and Frequent Plan for Small-Group Instruction
Week of _____

SMALL GROUP INSTRUCTION (LIST STUDENT NAMES IN EACH GROUP AND DAYS YOU MEET WITH THEM.)	FOCUS

Appendix C: Conferring Grid Template

Week of :

Math and Literacy

NAME: M			NAME: M			NAME: M		
		L			L			L

NAME: M			NAME: M			NAME: M		
		L			L			L

NAME: M			NAME: M			NAME: M		
		L			L			L

Appendix D: Spelling Tool

Aa	Bb	Cc
Dd	**Ee**	**Ff**
Gg	**Hh**	**Ii**
Jj **Kk**	**Ll**	**Mm**

Nn	Oo	Pp
Qq	Rr	Ss
Tt	Uu	Vv
Ww	Xx	Yy Zz

references

Bishop, Rudine Sims. 1990. "Mirrors, Windows and Sliding Glass Doors." *Perspectives: Choosing and Using Books for the Classroom* 6 (3): ix–xi.

Blevins, Wiley. 2016. *A Fresh Look at Phonics, Grades K-2: Common Causes of Failure and 7 Ingredients for Success*. Thousand Oaks, CA: Corwin.

Briceño, Allison, and Claudia Rodriguez-Mojica. 2022. *Conscious Classroom: Using Diverse Texts for Inclusion, Equity and Justice*. New Rochelle, NY: Benchmark Education.

Burkins, Jan, and Kari Yates. 2021. *Shifting the Balance: 6 Ways to Bring the Science of Reading into the Balanced Literacy Classroom*. Portsmouth, NH: Stenhouse.

Burkins, Jan and Kari Yates. n.d. "The Six Shifts." https://thesixshifts.com/.

"CORE Phonics Surveys." In *CORE, Assessing Reading: Multiple Measures*. 2nd ed. 2008. Arena Press. https://cdnsm5-ss10.sharpschool.com/UserFiles/Servers/Server_19566293/File/Academics/Exceptional%20Children%27s%20Services/CORE%20Phonics%20Survey.pdf.

Frazin, Shana, and Katy Wischow. 2019. *Unlocking the Power of Classroom Talk: Teaching Kids to Talk with Clarity & Purpose*. Portsmouth, NH: Heinemann.

Hattie, John. 2012. *Visible Learning for Teachers: Maximizing Impact on Learning*. New York: Routledge.

Harvard Office for Equity, Diversity, Inclusion and Belonging. 2024. "Heritage Months." https://edib.harvard.edu/heritage-months.

Iwasaki, Becky, Timothy Rasinski, Kasim Yildirim, and Belinda S. Zimmerman. 2013. "Let's Bring Back the Magic of Song for Teaching Reading." *The Reading Teacher* 67 (2): 137–141. www.timrasinski.com/presentations/article_iwasaki__rasinski__2013_.pdf.

Kilpatrick, David A. 2016. *Equipped for Reading Success: A Comprehensive, Step-by-Step for Developing Phonemic Awareness and Fluent Word Recognition*. North Syracuse, NY: Casey & Kirsch Publishers.

Learning for Justice. 2023. "Student Texts." www.learningforjustice.org/classroom-resources/texts?keyword=&field_grade_level%5B35%5D=35.

Liljedahl, Peter. 2020. *Building Thinking Classrooms in Mathematics, Grades K-12: 14 Teaching Practices for Enhancing Learning*. Thousand Oaks, CA: Corwin.

Martin, J.-P. 1985. Zum Aufbau didaktischer Teilkompetenzen beim Schüler. Fremdsprachenunterricht auf der lerntheoretischen Basis des Informationsverarbeitungsansatzes. Tübingen: Narr Verlag. Stollhans, S. (2015).

Mathis, Meghan. 2023. "The Big List of School-Appropriate Songs to Keep Everyone Pumped Up and Motivated." www.weareteachers.com/school-appropriate-songs.

Nichols, Maria. 2019. *Building Bigger Ideas: A Process for Teaching Purposeful Talk*. Portsmouth, NH: Heinemann.

Omohundro Wedekind, Kassia, and Christy Hermann Thompson. 2020. *Hands Down, Speak Out: Listening and Talking Across Literacy and Math*. Portsmouth, NH: Stenhouse.

Quimby, Melissa. 2024. "Meet Someone New Monday: Using Picture Book Biographies to Bring Marginalized Voices into the Classroom." Choice Literacy. https://choiceliteracy.com/article/meet-someone-new-monday-using-picture-book-biographies-to-bring-marginalized-voices-into-the-classroom/.

Rasinski, Timothy. 2016a. "Fry Instant Phrases." www.timrasinski.com/presentations/fry_600_instant_phrases.pdf

Rasinski, Timothy. 2016b. "Dr. Tim Rasinski on Implementing Reader's Theater." Literacy Connections. www.literacyconnections.com/rasinski-readers-theater-php/.

Rasinski, Timothy, and Chase Young. 2023. "A Step-by-Step Guide to Fluency Instruction in the Age of SOR." International Literacy Association webinar, April 26. https://ila.digitellinc.com/p/s/a-step-by-step-guide-to-fluency-instruction-in-the-age-of-sor-2432.

Richards, Regina G. 2024. "Making It Stick: Memorable Strategies to Enhance Learning." www.readingrockets.org/topics/reading-and-brain/articles/making-it-stick-memorable-strategies-enhance-learning.

Shatz, Itamar. 2024. "The Protégé Effect: How You Can Learn by Teaching Others—Effectiviology." Effectiviology. https://effectiviology.com/protege-effect-learn-by-teaching/.

Teachers College Reading and Writing Project. 2021. "A Tool for Supporting Moving Readers Up Levels." https://drive.google.com/file/d/1xx3Qq3gTrYs1W9wgLRDl3NqDiWdMUihE/view.

The One UN Climate Change Learning Partnership. 2024. "5 Young Environmental Activists Making a Difference in Climate Change." www.uncclearn.org/stories/5-young-environmental-activists-making-a-difference-in-climate-change/.

credits

index

Page numbers in *italics* indicate figures, **bold** a table

For Product Safety Concerns and Information please contact our EU
representative GPSR@taylorandfrancis.com
Taylor & Francis Verlag GmbH, Kaufingerstraße 24, 80331 München, Germany

www.ingramcontent.com/pod-product-compliance
Lightning Source LLC
Chambersburg PA
CBHW080555270326
41929CB00019B/3314